SEXUAL PROBLEMS
IN MARRIAGE

SEXUAL PROBLEMS IN MARRIAGE

Help from a Christian Counselor

by
F. PHILIP RICE

THE WESTMINSTER PRESS
Philadelphia

First edition

Published by The Westminster Press ®
Philadelphia, Pennsylvania

PRINTED IN THE UNITED STATES OF AMERICA
9 8 7 6 5 4 3 2 1

Library of Congress Cataloging in Publication Data

Rice, F. Philip.
  Sexual problems in marriage.

  Bibliography: p.
  1. Sex in marriage. 2. Sex therapy.
I. Title
HQ31.R46   613.9'5   77–27443
ISBN 0–664–24194–8

*To All Couples Who Want to Know
but Don't Know Where to Ask*

CONTENTS

Preface   9

I. HUMAN SEXUALITY

1. Sex, Love, and Happy Marriage   13
2. Some Typical Problems   22
3. Causes of Sexual Difficulties   33
4. Men, Women, and Their Sexual Response   48
5. Pleasuring and Lovemaking Techniques   65
6. Psychological Blocks to Sexual Response   77
7. Disturbed Marriage and Sexual Problems   95

II. DIFFERENCES IN SEXUAL PREFERENCES

8. Differences in the Desired Frequency
   of Sexual Relations   111
9. Differences in the Mode and Manner
   of Sexual Expression   124
10. Problems Over Adultery   136

(*Continued*)

III. MALE SEXUAL DYSFUNCTION

11. Premature Ejaculation   151

12. Impotence   160

13. Ejaculatory Incompetence   173

14. Low Sexual Drive   181

IV. FEMALE SEXUAL DYSFUNCTION

15. Female Frigidity   193

16. Orgasm Dysfunction   212

17. Dyspareunia (Painful Intercourse)
    and Vaginismus   229

V. SEX THERAPY

18. Getting Help   243

Bibliography   249

PREFACE

OVER twenty-five years of experience in marriage counseling and teaching have convinced me that sexual difficulties do more to wreck marriages than any other single cause. Many couples' life together in their twenty-five to fifty years of marriage is one of agony primarily because they lack a deeply satisfying sexual relationship.

Yet sexual problems can be solved. Troubled relationships can be improved. With sufficient knowledge and understanding, and sometimes with outside help, couples *can* find loving, pleasurable, and satisfying sexual experiences in marriage. They can learn to express their love through physical means and in ways that will enrich their marital union.

This book is written for all persons—both lay and professional—who seek a better understanding of the problems of sexual adjustment in marriage.

There are several characteristics that I have tried to incorporate into the book in order to make it as distinctive as possible—and not just another sex book.

One, much of the material is based upon the latest scientific knowledge and information as revealed by sex researchers and therapists. I have tried to utilize as much of this information as possible, but to describe it in nonmedical language so that it can be more easily understood by the average person.

Two, I have tried to illustrate throughout with real-life examples, drawn primarily from my own counseling and teaching experiences. I feel that such material is needed to add a note of reality to the discussion so that it becomes more than an academic exercise. The book deals with the problems of real people—who have feelings!

Three, the book deals very frankly with both the emotional *and* the physical or erotic components of sex. It is my conviction that love and sex ought to go together, that sex without love and love without sex is meaningless—for most married people. Certain chapters, such as "Pleasuring and Lovemaking Techniques," emphasize the importance of complete giving and of eroticism in sex, without, I hope, offense or overemphasis. It is my hope that such information, within the right context (loving marriage), will enable some persons who have negative feelings about sex to be freer to express their love in more intimate, uninhibited ways. But it is my hope also that readers will gain a better understanding of the importance of emotions and feelings if a sexual relationship is to be deeply satisfying and truly meaningful.

Four, this book is about sex in marriage, and so seeks to reflect and to encourage mature, sensitive, responsible, and moral sexual behavior. It is my conviction that sex without love, responsibility, and commitment is itself a major contributor to sexual difficulties such as frigidity, orgasm incapacity, or impotence.

Five, the chapter on adultery emphasizes that extramarital sexual relationships are both a symptom of deeper problems in marriage and a problem in and of themselves. Adultery is a symptom that a marriage is breaking, or is already broken, and is itself a leading cause of marital breakups as well as personal heartache.

And six, because many marital problems cannot be solved by couples themselves, I have tried to offer some practical guidance on where to get help.

F.P.R.

Cape Elizabeth, Maine

PART I

HUMAN SEXUALITY

1

SEX, LOVE,
AND HAPPY MARRIAGE

EXPERTS like Masters and Johnson, directors of the Reproductive Biology Research Foundation in St. Louis, estimate
that half of all married couples have some problems relating
to sex. Some of these problems are minor and can be overcome easily with proper information or help. But others of
these problems are serious enough to make the couple miser-
able, or even to wreck their marriage completely.

One reason so many adults have problems is that most
persons who are now over twenty-one years of age grew up
during years of sexual suppression and ignorance, when sex
was considered only a dirty word and not something that
curious boys and girls, or even adult men and women, had
any right to know anything about. Information that was available through the underground press, in stag movies, or at
local drugstores was often confusing, misleading, and plainly
inadequate or untrue. The modern sex education movement
in the public schools did not really become very widespread
until the 1960s and even then its establishment caused considerable furor. Also, there had been almost no scientific
research on human sexual response until Masters and Johnson published the results of their work. Their book *Human
Sexual Response* was dated 1966, the first of its kind ever
published. Their second work, *Human Sexual Inadequacy,*
didn't come out until 1970. The Supreme Court decisions on
obscenity did not release the flood of sex-oriented, often pornographic literature and movies until the late 1960s. One

reason for the deluge of this type of material was that American boys and girls during the two hundred years of the country's bicentennial had been growing up quite ignorant of the basic facts of life. One can't really blame them for satisfying their curiosity which had so long been squelched.

The real tragedy, of course, is that much of the sex-oriented material which is tawdry is also misleading, unscientific, and untrue. Instead of getting helpful information from pornography, couples are becoming even more confused. The other part of the story is that much of the unscientific literature takes sex out of the context of a loving, caring relationship and emphasizes only the need for human flesh to massage human flesh in order to achieve an erotic response. Nothing could be more misleading than this idea. One of the most important emphases of Masters and Johnson and of other knowledgeable therapists is the role of emotions and feelings in either blocking or releasing sexual responses. By emphasizing only the biological aspects of sex, pornographic literature omits the most important part: the importance of feelings of warmth, real concern, trust, and love. Sex is more than biology, but one would never know it by going into an X-rated movie or bookstore.

This is not to say that biology is unimportant in achieving a satisfying sexual relationship in marriage. It is most important to know, understand, and be able to use biological facts and information in one's lovemaking. Couples can be taught to enjoy the physical sensations of sex: to experience the rhythmic pulses of orgasm, to respond to the physical sensations of being caressed, to learn the pleasure and warmth of being physically close to one's naked mate with whom one can share intimate caresses. There is pleasure in physical sight, touch, sound, and even in smell.

But sex is more than mechanical manipulation or rhythmic movements, however skillfully performed. It is more than flesh rubbing on flesh, as some adult movies would have us believe. Popular literature gives the impression that all couples have to do to have a happy sexual life is to have sexual intercourse frequently, engage in uninhibited love play, have mutual orgasms, show variety and imagination in their technique (like making love in a bathtub of Jell-O), and they will be satisfied. Such is simply not true. Couples can find physical stimulation and release, and even come to a mutual agreement about the mode and manner of their sexual life, but still find "something lacking." The something lacking is often warmth of feeling, depth of emotion, and closeness of spirit. The something can only be described as emotional and spiritual: oneness, tenderness, a kind of secure awareness that one is accepted and loved without limit, and that one has expressed the deepest feelings of concern, sympathy, kindness, affection, and unselfishness of which one is capable.

There is a considerable amount of research which, on the surface, shows that women want and need these emotional and spiritual components to sex, but that men do not. In summary, the studies show that the majority of women have sex, but with love, and that the majority of men will have sex even without love. As a result of these findings, the studies suggest: women are more emotionally oriented than men in their sexual desires; men are more erotically oriented in the pursuit of sex than are women.

What the studies don't go on to say, however, is that men who have sex repeatedly without any mutuality of feeling are the first to admit that sex begins to become an empty experience because of the lack of emotional involvement. After the novelty of physical excitement wears off, they find that there is nothing left. Men, like women, prefer meaningful relationships. There are many men who wouldn't think of having sex with a prostitute or with anyone other than the woman they love. Even those men who do visit prostitutes want them to pretend involvement and feign affection. If the prostitute does not, the men don't like it, and so seek out someone else.

Men and women are not really that different. Differences that exist are largely the result of cultural conditioning. Women are still reared to believe that it is only right to give themselves sexually to the man they love, whereas men are still reared to try to prove their manhood through sexual prowess, to prove their machismo, their masculinity. As a consequence, men and women do express their sexuality somewhat differently. However, most men have just as great a need for closeness, tenderness, real concern, sympathetic understanding, and affection as do women. They have been taught to suppress their feelings, but the needs are still there. Else why are so many men attracted to warm, maternal, tender, and understanding women? It is my firm conviction that men want their deepest emotional needs fulfilled in their sexual relationships. When these needs are not satisfied, men do feel that "something is lacking."

At the same time, modern research has revealed that not only do women want love and affection but that they also want sex: beautifully erotic, wonderfully pleasurable and uninhibited sex, and that after generations of repression they have discovered their sexuality and found they can enjoy sex as much as any man. Many women have even a greater capacity than men have. They are often multiorgasmic, whereas most men can have only a single orgasm. Once their inhibitions are broken down, women can love sex as much as they desire love, just as a man can desire love as much as he wants sex.

The task of the couple, therefore, is to cultivate love, and then to learn to use the body as a means of expressing inner feelings, emotions, and sexual urges. In this sense, sex has a sacramental function, to be a physical means of expressing an inward grace. When sex is thus lifted above the level of just physical expression and response, it becomes most satisfying to human beings.

But the important question of this chapter still remains: What is the relationship between sex and a happy marriage, and can one be happily married without a satisfying sex life? What is the relationship?

We must not forget that what is satisfying to one couple may not be at all acceptable to another. Human beings differ tremendously in their sexual appetites, in the manner and means by which they want to enjoy sex, and in their sexual habits and aims. What satisfies one couple may not be completely fulfilling to another. If both the husband and the wife are happy with their marriage without any sexual involvement at all, then, to them, they have a good marriage, even though most couples would find it a very frustrating experience. There are couples who want intercourse every day, or several times a day. Other couples would find this frequency completely unacceptable. The point is, if both the husband and the wife are satisfied with their sex life, it can contribute in a positive way to their overall marital happiness, but if the couple disagree, or if one or both are frustrated or unhappy with their sexual relationship, it can significantly reduce or even destroy marital satisfaction.

One interesting study showed that 60 percent of the wives who rated their marriages as very happy reached orgasm 90 to 100 percent of the time in coitus. Thirty-eight percent of the wives who rated their marriages as very unhappy never or rarely reached orgasm (only 1 to 9 percent of the time) in coitus. (Gebhard, 1966) These findings suggest a positive correlation between marital happiness and sexual orgasm. They tend to be found together. However, the same study also showed that 4 percent of the wives who rated their marriage as very happy never had orgasms, and that 38 percent of the wives who rated their marriages as very unhappy practically always had orgasms. It is obvious that orgasm response did not ensure that wives would have a happy marriage, nor did happy marriage always result in orgasms. Nevertheless, *it was harder for wives to be happily married without orgasm, and it was harder to have an orgasm without a happy marriage.*

The results of this study should not be surprising, since sex is one of the strongest drives with which human beings are endowed. When couples marry, they fully expect that their sexual needs will be met. If they are not met, tension, frustration, anger, or hurt is the result.

The author was called upon to counsel with a married

couple who were having sexual difficulties. The following is from his notes of the interview.

The wife did not seem to be too interested in sex, even though her husband was. When the husband approached her, she would either try to repulse him or make the experience so unpleasant that he wouldn't like it. Very typically she would take off all her clothes, throw herself onto the bed, and exclaim: "Hurry up and get it over with." This made the husband furious.

After several weeks of counseling, the wife was called to jury duty to sit in on a murder trial of a husband who had brutally mutilated his wife with a butcher knife. He had cut off her breasts, and repeatedly stabbed her in the genital area. Day after day, this female jurist had to sit in the courtroom listening to the husband tell how he really loved his wife, but had killed her in a moment of rage after she had refused to have intercourse with him for a number of years. As might be expected, the woman jurist was most upset by the trial.

After the trial was over she came back for counseling. Her first words were: "I never really realized before how much sex could mean to my husband. I really thought it did not matter to him, any more than it mattered to me, and that he was just nagging me about it to make me angry. I don't know how much of a lover I can be, but at least I want to try."

And try she did, and very successfully. Within only two weeks, with patience and sufficient motivation, this woman was fully orgasmic, and enjoyed sex for the first time with her husband. The story illustrates very well the power and strength of the sexual drive and its importance for benefit or harm in the marriage relationship.

It is very difficult to accept rejection, especially from one's mate. The husband who refuses to sleep with his wife even though he says he loves her may really be saying: "I love you but I don't like sex." But the wife interprets the refusal as a rejection of her. "If you really loved me, you would want to make love to me." She is hurt because her husband has refused her. If refusal comes often, she not only becomes more hurt, she now begins to be angry as her resentment grows. Conflict develops, grows, and becomes more bitter if the situation continues. Eventually, the wife may develop such negative feelings toward her husband that she certainly doesn't want to sleep with him. If the husband also becomes hostile, he may start withholding sex as a means of getting back at her. She may even start demanding sex as a means of punishing him, because she knows it will make him angry. So sex becomes an expression of anger and hostility rather than of love.

But let us suppose the situation is reversed: the wife doesn't particularly like sex, but the husband does, and since she wants to please him, she makes loves with him because she knows he wants to. The husband is appreciative, feels more affectionate toward her because they have slept together, and feels everything is right with the marriage. If this situation is repeated often enough, however, the wife begins to resent her martyr role and feels that her husband uses her selfishly without regard for her feelings. She begins to feel that "if he loved me, he would consider my feelings and not make so many sexual demands upon me." Her resentment grows, which she begins to take out on her husband in little ways: through verbal digs, nagging criticism, or by refusing to do things for him that he requests or that he enjoys. Eventually she may object so much to her passive role in their sexual relationship that she begins to make excuses so she won't have to submit to his sexual advances. At times she starts arguments so he will get mad and stomp out of the house, thereby letting her alone, which gives her some relief, but little real comfort. In this case, the wife has assumed that sex is a responsibility which she dutifully performs, but at the expense of her own feelings and emotional health. Eventually, this solution too may wreck what might have been an otherwise good marriage.

What is the answer? Certainly, to try to forget about the problems is no solution. To refuse to talk about them, or to refuse to try to solve them, makes matters worse. Problems of sexual maladjustment that remain unsolved continue to be an impediment to emotional closeness and harmonious marriage. In both of the above examples, the problems might have been solved before they became this serious. These couples were not able to work things out themselves, they needed outside help. At other times, through discussion, reading, practice, and experience, couples solve their problems very nicely. The important requirement is for couples to be willing to try, to recognize that sex can be a chief contributor to a happy marriage or a powerful force that can destroy it.

There are people who have been reared with very negative ideas about sex, so that normal feelings have been repressed. They have sexual problems, not because they have a "bad" marriage, but because of the way they were brought up. But they can learn to respond and to enjoy their sexuality. Many people do not have much scientific knowledge and understanding of the biology of sexual stimulation and response, but they can learn to be expert lovers if they are willing. Others have very wholesome feelings about sex, and a lot of scientific knowledge gained from good reading, but they need practice. Their initial efforts will be clumsy, but they can learn. One study showed that wives who were virgins at the time of marriage but who had very accepting, mature feelings about sex did not have as good a sex adjustment in the beginning of marriage as wives who were sexually experienced before marriage. But in only two months' time the virginal wives had caught up with the more experienced women. Experience can be gained. The important thing is the desire to learn and to try. Most couples can work out sexual problems with help, and with sufficient motivation.

Sexual difficulties are among the leading marital problems that couples face and they often persist after twenty years of marriage. But this does not mean that this situation has to be accepted. Apparently, couples find it easier to work out problems relating to money, in-laws, friends, religion, or rearing children than those relating to sex. But one reason has been the cloak of ignorance surrounding sex. Another reason has been the lack of available help with sexual difficulties. In the past it was easier to find someone to help them work out a budget than it was to find someone to help them have an orgasm.

But this picture is slowly changing. A great deal of scientific information is now available. More and more specialists are being trained in helping couples with sexual dysfunctions. Knowledge of the causes and symptoms of these sexual problems and of how the problems are treated is increasing. The purpose of this book is to share a part of this knowledge so that couples who are having problems will understand them better and be motivated to do something about them. The book should also meet the needs of professionals who want to learn more about the new and exciting developments in this field. A final purpose is for all of us to gain a clearer, deeper understanding and acceptance of ourselves as sexual beings.

2

SOME TYPICAL PROBLEMS

SEXUAL DYSFUNCTION

The human reproductive system, which includes the sex organs, is an amazing system. Consider, for example, the fact that mere thoughts can produce sexual reactions. A man can start thinking about sex and have an erection. A woman can read a romantic story and dream about a man making love to her. A glance at a sensuous picture may produce blushing, an increase in the respiratory rate or in the blood pressure.

Under most circumstances, the body functions quite smoothly. It reacts in predictable ways to certain stimuli brought to it. If a woman's breast is caressed, the nipples become engorged and firm. If a man's penis is stimulated in a pleasurable way, it becomes erect. If it is stimulated enough, an ejaculation occurs. These are predictable, normal reactions to sexual stimuli.

Sometimes, however, difficulties arise, so that the sex organs do not respond as they should. The penis is rubbed and it doesn't get hard. The breast is stimulated and the nipples don't become enlarged and erect. A couple copulate for a long period of time and the husband and wife don't reach a climax. Obviously, something has gone wrong, so that the expected response is not produced by a particular stimuli.

When this happens, the condition is called a *sexual dysfunction*, which really means a malfunctioning of the human sexual response system. It means that a person hasn't reacted as one would normally expect. Some of the problems discussed in this book represent examples of sexual dysfunction. Part of these are male dysfunction; others are female dysfunction. Let's get an overall view first of some common male sexual dysfunctions.

MALE SEXUAL DYSFUNCTION

Premature Ejaculation. *Premature ejaculation* may be defined as the inability to delay ejaculation long enough for the man to place his penis within the vagina and to continue intercourse and thrusting long enough for the woman to have an orgasm 50 percent of the time. This definition assumes that the woman can ordinarily have an orgasm, and that when she doesn't, it is because of the rapidity of the male's ejaculation. The definition implies that the male is unable to exert voluntary control over the timing of his ejaculation and that he comes too quickly. One wife described her experience in this way:

> When George and I were married, neither of us were experienced. We hadn't gone out much, and didn't have much opportunity. I was nervous about everything, since I was a virgin. I went to a doctor; he examined me and said I had a very thick hymen and that if I had any trouble, to let him know. I'm ashamed to say it, but George and I didn't even know how to do it, even though we tried. Every time he started to enter, he'd come and then he couldn't do it anymore.
>
> One night we were feeling pretty good—we'd been out drinking. George did get inside of me. I bled an awful lot. After that, George would do it the regular way, but he comes in only a minute or so, just about the time I'm getting warmed up. The only way I can get satisfied is for him to finish me off by hand. I like it, and George doesn't mind, but I'd like to be able to come when we're joined together. George kisses me and loves me, but it's like he's too far away. It's like we're not close enough when we're not joined together.

In this example, the problem was with George, not with his wife, Betty, even though it was she who was unable to reach a climax during coitus. George was young and virile. His wife was attractive and he became aroused by her very quickly, so much so that he was unable to delay his climax long enough for her to have an orgasm too. George's problem of premature ejaculation is one of the most common with which young couples are faced. It is, however, one of the easiest problems to overcome with proper help.

Impotence. Another of the more common problems with male sexual functioning is the problem of *impotence.* Impotence should not be confused with sterility. A man who is sterile is unable to conceive children. When he is impotent, he is unable to produce an erection so that coital connection can take place, or he is unable to maintain an erection long enough to complete the sexual act. Mrs. G. told of her marital disappointment.

> From the very beginning of our marriage, I noticed that Bob had trouble getting hard. Sometimes he would, and sometimes he wouldn't. I could never tell ahead of time when it would happen. Sometimes he would get hard, but only for a minute or so: long enough for him to finish, but not me. Sometimes he would wake up in the morning with an erection; we'd hurry up and begin, but as soon as he entered, he'd get soft again. It's very frustrating. I asked him if he used to have that trouble, and he said he never did until he married me. He tries to make me believe that it's my fault, that I'm doing something wrong, but I think there is something wrong with him.

Sometimes a man has never been able to achieve and/or maintain an erection quality sufficient to accomplish a successful coital connection. This condition is known as *primary impotence,* which means that it has always existed. In other cases, a man develops *secondary impotence.* In this case, there has been at least one instance and sometimes there have been dozens or hundreds of times when erection has been sufficient to have successful intercourse. Then one or more episodes of erective failure occur.

In recent years, physicians have become increasingly aware of the problem of impotence. Doctors at college student health centers report increasing numbers of men coming in for treatment. It may be that the increasing numbers brought to the attention of physicians is a result of more men being willing to talk about their difficulty and to get help. Fortunately, the condition is treatable in the great majority of cases.

Ejaculatory Incompetence. A minority of males also suffer from *ejaculatory incompetence.* In this difficulty, the male gets excited quite normally, has a firm erection, and is able to have normal intercourse, but is not able to reach a climax. As a result, intercourse becomes frustrating. Even though he desires an orgasm, and his stimulation is enough to trigger a climax, he cannot come. This condition is in contrast to that of the impotent man who may be able to ejaculate with a limp penis, if he is sufficiently stimulated. Ejaculatory incompetence is quite rare, although most men experience some occasions when they have difficulty having an orgasm.

Low Sexual Drive. Strangely enough, one sees very little reference in the literature to the fact of a *low sexual drive,* or even almost nonexistent sexual drive, in men. Female frigidity is discussed at length, but very little reference is made to men who are frigid as indicated by their lack of desire for sexual relations. Most men have an ample sexual drive, a persistent desire for regular intercourse, and a healthy sexual appetite. But there are a minority of males who have a low sexual drive, who seldom take any interest in sexual expression. While in the minority, these cases are not at all unusual. When they do occur, they create a great deal of misery for the wife. Mrs. B. is in her forties and had been married fifteen years when she told this story.

My problem is that my husband doesn't want to go to bed with me. When we were courting, he wanted sex every time we were together, but the last several years he's been less and less interested. Would you believe it, we haven't had intercourse in a whole year? He comes home, eats dinner, gets into bed to watch television, and then turns over to go to sleep. If I say anything, he says he's tired, that he has to go to work in the morning. I'm tired sometimes; I go to work too, but that doesn't keep me from wanting sex with my husband. I've tried everything: cooking special meals—last night I even served dinner by candlelight. I bought a really sexy nightgown, but it didn't help any. Ralph turned over and went to sleep as usual. I said something, then he got real mad and accused me of being a nympho. That started the whole fight. I don't know what I'm going to do. I certainly don't want to live like this.

These four problems—*premature ejaculation, impotence, ejaculatory incompetence,* and a *low sexual drive*—are all examples of male sexual dysfunction. Each of them will be discussed in detail in separate chapters of this book.

FEMALE SEXUAL DYSFUNCTION

There are four principal types of female sexual dysfunction. These are *female frigidity, orgasm dysfunction, painful intercourse (dyspareunia),* and *vaginismus.*

Female Frigidity. Frigidity may be defined as a lack of desire for or a lack of pleasure in sexual relations. One husband related:

My wife is not at all interested in sex. She never has been from the beginning of marriage. Even on our honeymoon she wanted to go sight-seeing, out to dinner, or to the movies. She ran me around everywhere. I wanted to make love, but she always wanted to do something else. I think we had intercourse only three times on our honeymoon, but when we did, she didn't seem to enjoy it. She let me make love to her, but she lay there hardly moving, like she wasn't even involved. Once she said to me: "If you hurry, we can catch the nine o'clock movie." That really made me wonder. Since then I'm lucky if I can talk her into it once a month. When I suggest going to bed, she accuses me of being a sex maniac. "All you're interested in is sex," she says. Sure I'm interested, especially since I don't get much. I'd like to have relations a couple of times a week, but she wouldn't. She always makes excuses. She has a headache; she wants to watch a special television show; or she has to get up early in the morning. I can't make love during her period, but I can't make love after it either, because she's too worn out from losing so much blood. During the middle of the month, she's worried she'll get pregnant.

Sometimes she makes me feel terrible. She tells me: "Get out of here and let me alone." Several times I cried myself to sleep. She didn't know it. She makes me feel that sex is the dirtiest thing there is, and that I'm abnormal. She makes me feel like she hates me. I'm her husband—I don't think that's right, but I don't know if she is ever going to change.

Female frigidity may manifest itself in ways different from the previous example. In that case, the wife just refused to have intercourse most of the time. In other cases, the wife is willing; she wants to go to bed with her husband because she wants to please him, but she doesn't really derive much pleasure from the experience. Sex is like brushing her teeth or combing her hair. It's something that has to be done.

In some instances, the woman is responsive in the beginning of marriage but becomes frigid later on because of lack of pleasure in the experience or because of things that happen in the couple's relationship. Thus, frigidity may be *primary*, where the woman has never derived erotic pleasure with any partner in any situation, or it can be *secondary*, where the woman has reponded to some extent on at least one occasion, but is frigid, or becomes so, on other occasions.

Orgasm Dysfunction. Sometimes the wife gets aroused to a certain point, but not beyond that point, so that she can reach a climax. This problem, referred to as *orgasm dysfunction,* is one of the most common in women. Only a minority of women have never had an orgasm *(primary orgasmic dysfunction).* Most are orgastic occasionally, or usually, or used to be but aren't now *(secondary orgasmic dysfunction).* A minority have an orgasm every time they have intercourse. A counselor gave this summary of the marital sexual life of Mr. and Mrs. M.:

> They had been married over three years and had sex on the average of once or twice a week during that time. Mrs. M. remained completely nonorgastic. She never masturbated before marriage, at least to the point of orgasm. She said that her husband stimulates her and that she becomes somewhat aroused during the experience, but that she has trouble relaxing and letting herself go. When she gets worked up to a certain point, she begins to feel uncomfortable, wants her husband to enter, and to complete the act, which he does at her urging.
>
> The couple had adjusted fairly well to the situation as it existed, especially Mrs. M., but Mr. M. said he'd rather have his wife enjoy sex completely. He felt sorry that he could have a climax and she couldn't. It was at his urging that they came in for help.

Painful Intercourse (Dyspareunia). Another common female difficulty is when intercourse is painful (called *dyspareunia*). "It hurts" is a common complaint to gynecologists. The pain may be severe or slight, the degree depending upon its origin and the woman's condition. While such a difficulty is not unusual, it is not "natural." Except for intercourse in the early days of marriage, or under certain other conditions, such as too soon after childbirth, it should not be painful. Pain indicates that something is wrong and needs attention, usually that of a physician.

Vaginismus. Most people have heard of couples getting "stuck together." Actually, such stories are fictional. Dogs and some other animals get stuck together, but not people. When a male dog becomes sexually aroused, a bulb at the base of the penis swells up, locking the penis within the vagina. This is nature's way of ensuring proper deposition of the sperm, since the male ejaculates over a period of time, not in a few seconds as in human males. In human beings, so the fiction goes, couples are discovered in the act of intercourse, or the woman becomes frightened suddenly, so her vaginal muscles contract and lock her to the male. Always, the story goes, a doctor and an ambulance have to be called to take them to the hospital to get "unstuck."

Such situations don't happen. What does happen, however, is that anxiety, fear, or some psychological problem can cause the muscles of the vagina to constrict, involuntarily, either preventing the male from entering or causing so much discomfort for the woman that to continue intercourse is impossible. This problem, which is rather rare, is called *vaginismus*. It is the involuntary contraction and spasm of the muscles of the vagina.

DIFFERENCES IN SEXUAL PREFERENCES

In addition to the problems that occur within the response mechanisms of individuals, there are other types of problems that arise because of differences in sexual preferences between a particular man and woman. The husband and the wife each respond in a typical fashion, but their sexual preferences are dissimilar, so that problems arise because they have differences as a couple. For example, a husband wants intercourse in the morning, a wife likes it at night. Both desires are quite usual; a problem arises only because the husband and the wife are not in agreement. A large number of sexual problems arise because of such differences. Let us consider some of these differences.

Differences in Desired Frequency of Sexual Relations. A particular couple may have differences in their *sexual appetite*.

That is, there is a difference in frequency with which they desire sexual relations. One person may want intercourse three times a week; the other is satisfied with twice a month. One wife complained:

> My husband and I argue all the time because he thinks he has to have sex four or five times a week. He would rather have sex than eat. I am of the opinion that there's more to marriage than that. I'm not against sex, but twice a week is more than enough. I don't even think he enjoys it sometimes. It's as though he forces himself.

Actually, of course, there is no optimum number of times per week or month that couples *should* have sexual intercourse. What suits them is the important thing. A problem arises only when they differ in desired frequency. Frustration arises when intercourse is too seldom. But a person can also feel used, or abused, and develop considerable resentment if he or she feels pushed into sexual relations more often than desired.

Differences in Mode and Manner of Sexual Expression. Couples may manifest distinct preferences and differences in the way they would like to enjoy sex. In recent years, oral-genital contact as a method of stimulation has become much more common. However, individuals differ widely in their acceptance of the practice. Such was the case of one couple in their early thirties. The wife described the problem:

> For the past several weeks my husband has wanted me to put my mouth on him. It all started when he read a trashy magazine which he picked up. He says that a lot of couples do this, and that there is nothing wrong with it. I'm not a prude, but the whole idea disgusts me. When I don't do it, he gets mad and we have a fight. Is he sick or am I?

Actually, neither the husband nor the wife is sick. Since the majority of couples now engage in some form of oral-genital sex, the practice can be considered quite normal. In the previous example, it is the disagreement which creates the problem, not whether they do or they don't have oral sex.

In contrast to oral-genital sex in which a majority of couples participate, the practice of mate-swapping, or "swinging," is greatly in the minority. When the subject is brought up and one person objects, as many do, a real problem arises.

My husband and I have been going with another couple that are real swingers. We've seen a lot of one another lately and the other husband has started to get familiar. Also, his wife has started to hang all over John. When I objected about this to my husband, he said that he and the other husband had talked and they would like to swap wives. He asked me if I wanted to. The idea never occurred to me; I was really shocked. John has been trying to talk me into it, but I told him there's no deal.

Differences between mates over desired forms of sexual expression are not always as serious as this, but minor disagreements can create difficulties nonetheless. One difference is when to have intercourse. One husband wanted to have sex in the morning before going to work. He said he was too tired at night. The wife wanted to have sex at night. She was too busy in the morning getting the kids off to school. In another situation, the husband refused to engage in love play with his wife, because he described it as masturbation, which, he said, "is not right; it is queer." Another differed on the lighting in the room. The husband wanted the light on. He liked to see his wife naked. She wanted the light off. She was too embarrassed. Another couple argued over positions in intercourse. The wife wanted to try different ways: she liked to be on top; he liked it better when she was on the bottom. She wanted to try anal intercourse. He thought it was disgusting.

There is no end to the differences that couples can have. But such differences themselves are not as important as whether or not the couple are able to work them out.

Adultery or extramarital sexual relations with or without the knowledge or approval of one's mate continue to create problems for many couples, and deserve close attention in a separate chapter.

SUMMARY

PRINCIPAL PROBLEMS THAT COUPLES FACE

Male Sexual Dysfunction

> Premature ejaculation
> Impotence
> Ejaculatory incompetence
> Low sexual drive

Female Sexual Dysfunction

> Female frigidity
> Orgasm dysfunction
> Dyspareunia (painful intercourse)
> Vaginismus

Differences in Sexual Preferences

> Differences in desired frequency of sexual relations
> Differences in the mode and manner of sexual expression
> Problems over adultery

3

CAUSES
OF SEXUAL DIFFICULTIES

BEFORE getting into a detailed discussion of specific problems, let's take a look at some of the causes of these difficulties. In general, all sexual dysfunctions have either physical or emotional causes, or both. From a purely physical point of view, sex involves many other organs besides just the penis and the vagina. The brain and the nervous system carry the mental images and physical stimuli to the sexual organs. The heart and the circulatory system are involved, since under sexual excitement the heart beats faster and increases the pulse rate and the blood pressure. Particular blood vessels in the sexual organs of both male and female constrict, preventing blood from escaping as fast as it flows in so the surrounding tissues become erect. The lungs are involved: breathing becomes faster and more labored when the person is sexually excited. The muscles of the neck, abdomen, chest, arms, legs, and pelvis grow tense. The body moves rhythmically during intercourse. The hands and the mouth may be employed in tactical stimulation. What we're saying is that sexual response is a very complex physiological process involving much of the physical body. For this reason, what happens to the whole body or any part of it may affect one's sexual life. A person who is ill, or just very tired, for example, may not be able to respond sexually.

But sexual expression also involves one's feelings or emotions. In fact, the emotional component of sex is so important that feelings themselves can have a definite effect upon physical response. Feelings of love and affection can stimulate sexual response and pleasure. Worry, fear, or disgust may completely inhibit sexual feelings. In fact, the body can be functioning quite normally and healthily, but when negative feelings or an emotional upset occur, the sexual response may be blocked. Therefore, in talking about the causes of sexual difficulties, one must also discuss any and all factors that relate to feelings: how persons feel about themselves, their bodies, their sexual organs, or how they feel about sex itself or about their sexual partner. Negative feelings in relation to any one of these things may inhibit sexual expression.

This makes an examination of the causes of sexual problems a complicated subject. For purposes of clarity of discussion, these causes will be grouped into five categories.

Ignorance. A lack of knowledge and understanding of sexual anatomy, sexual response, and lovemaking techniques may be the reason why couples have problems. People aren't born with an understanding of male and female differences or of how to make love.

Inadequate stimulation. Sexual responses may not occur because the individual has not been stimulated properly in the right places, in an appropriate way, for a long enough time.

Psychological blocks. Negative attitudes about sex, the human body, the sexual organs, about being male or female, or toward oneself or the other persons may inhibit response. Fear and anxiety can create problems. A fear of pregnancy, of being hurt, of rejection, of failure, or even of doing something pleasurable are common causes of difficulties, as are feelings of guilt or disgust.

Negative feelings toward one's partner, or a disturbance in the relationship. People respond best to those they love, admire, and trust. Contrary feelings can influence their ability to give themselves to one another. This is why the quality and the emotional tone of a couple's relationship are important to their sexual life.

Physical causes. As has been mentioned, since sexual response involves many parts of the body, what affects the body may influence the ability to respond sexually. Physical abnormalities, various illnesses, general ill-health, or medication and drugs may be important causes of sexual difficulties. Each of these five problems will be examined in more detail.

IGNORANCE AND LACK OF KNOWLEDGE

Experiments have been conducted in which sexually mature male and female monkeys are placed together in the same cage. After a brief period of getting acquainted, they begin to show sexual interest in each other. They embrace and caress each other, touch each other's genitals, become increasingly agitated and excited and show interest in coitus. But it is only after considerable trial and error that they learn how to copulate. They have the interest, but not the inborn knowledge of how to have intercourse. Human beings are similar. Sexual instinct and urges are inborn, but a knowledge of lovemaking is not. This must be learned.

In spite of the flood of sexual literature that has reached the newsstands, many people are still woefully ignorant of the basic facts of life.

Recently, a bride-to-be went to her physician to discuss sex in marriage. The girl was anxious because she had looked at herself while squatting over a mirror and was afraid that she was too small to receive her husband's penis. She wanted to know how big a penis was. When told, she was even more worried, because her urine came out in only a narrow stream and she was certain that the opening would never be big enough for a penis to fit in. The doctor explained to her that she had three openings down there: one, the anus, out of which feces passed; a second, very small opening, the urethra, out of which urine came; and a third, much larger opening, the vagina, which received the penis in intercourse and through which a baby passed when being born. As far as the girl was concerned, however, she thought she must be abnormal because she had found only two openings (she actually found the anus and the vagina which she mistook for the urethra but thought the urine came out of the vaginal orifice).

Such an incident illustrates the fact that even in our modern age many persons are woefully uninformed about basic sexual facts. While there are many books and magazines on the market that deal with various phases of human sexuality, some contain information that is very unscientific and quite misleading. One recent issue of a screen magazine had an article about the evils of masturbation and how it would harm one's sexual life. Even if such sources get their facts correct, which this screen magazine didn't, they thrive on sensationalism and often teach attitudes and feelings about sex that are hardly conducive to loving and responsible sexual behavior between two married persons who care for each other. Many emphasize sadistic, violent sex, group sex, extramarital sex, or only the physical aspects of sex with very little thought about the important emotional components of satisfying sexual relationships. Such literature, by distorting the nature and uses of sex, actually doesn't help couples to work out their difficulties.

The author has been involved over the years in teaching marriage courses to college youths and in sex education of both adults and children. Today's youths, although more permissive and open about sex than their parents, are not necessarily better informed. Here are some sample questions asked in a college class:

"The girls in our dorm say it is all right to have intercourse with a boy up to five times and you won't get pregnant, but after that you have to start to worry. Is this true?"

"How does a girl know when she has an orgasm?"

"What is the safe period of the month when you can't get pregnant?"

"What is the clitoris?"

"How do you turn a girl on?"

"Do girls come like fellows do?"

"Do girls get wet dreams?"

"How can you tell if you're pregnant?"

"Is it all right to have intercourse in the morning?"

"If a woman can't have a baby, can she still have intercourse?"

"Can you tell if a girl is a virgin or not?"

"Can you get syphilis from a toilet seat?"

A few years ago the author was involved in counseling an unmarried college sophomore who was seven months pregnant. Her friends had become concerned and reported the situation to the college physician, who examined her and found her with child. The girl was completely surprised. "We only did it once, how could I be pregnant?" was her question. I asked her if she had wondered about why her period stopped. Her reply was: "A lot of my girl friends are irregular." I asked her if she had felt the baby kick. "I thought I had gas," was her reply. When I mentioned her enlarging abdomen, she replied: "I thought I was getting fat."

Such incidents seem incredible in this day and age, but they are not at all uncommon. Even if individuals understand the basic facts of reproduction, some have only a superficial understanding of sexual intercourse and of how to make love. One bride was married for a year before she knew that anything was supposed to happen during intercourse. She would get a little excited, but was never orgasmic, and really didn't know she was supposed to be. Another bride commented:

No one ever explained anything at all to me. I didn't know anything about what I was supposed to do when we made love.

It is no wonder that so many couples have problems with sexual adjustments.

INADEQUATE STIMULATION

Lack of stimulation is another major cause of sexual difficulties. If the individual man or woman is not stimulated in the right places, in an acceptable manner, and for a long enough period of time, sufficient arousal never takes place so that orgasm occurs. One wife complained:

> I really don't enjoy sex with my husband, because I don't get anything out of it. The reason is, Chuck never really tries to arouse me by kissing me or playing with me. I've tried to tell him that I need time to get worked up, that he has to caress me and pet with me first, but he gets worked up so quickly that he wants to hurry and enter before he comes. Afterward, he's not interested.

In this situation, the husband was too inconsiderate of his wife's feelings and needs to take the time to arouse her sufficiently before coital connection took place.

Insufficient arousal through foreplay is one of the primary causes of orgasm dysfunction in women. One research study at the Institute for Sex Research showed the relationship between duration of foreplay and a wife's orgasm rate. (Gebhard, 1966) When foreplay took place from 1 to 10 minutes, only two fifths of the wives reached orgasm nearly always, but when foreplay was 21 minutes or more, nearly three fifths of the wives achieved this high orgasm rate. This same study showed also the relationship between the duration of penile intromission (the length of time the penis was in the vagina) and the female orgasm rate. When intromission was under one minute, wives achieved orgasm in only slightly over one quarter of the occasions when they made love, while intromission of 1 to 11 minutes resulted in an orgasm rate of over 50 percent of all the coital connections. (Gebhard, 1966) Arousal takes time. Lovemaking that is rushed because of the pressure of time may be completely frustrating. Human beings are not machines that function sexually by time clocks. The couple who are late for work and try to hurry up may find that nothing significant or satisfying happens, so that the whole episode becomes a source of frustration.

Some young women enter marriage sexually unawakened —that is, they have never been sufficiently aroused to have experienced orgasm. They have never masturbated or petted to orgasm, nor have they had sexual intercourse. They certainly have the capacity to respond, but really don't know what their husbands should do to arouse them. If the husband is awkward, inexperienced, or inconsiderate, and if the wife is shy and can't suggest to him what really feels good, she may not become aroused at all. Sex therapists have discovered that the woman who has masturbated to orgasm prior to marriage is much more likely to be orgasmic in the first months of marriage than the one who has never masturbated. The reason is that once a woman experiences orgasm, at least she knows more about what to expect and how to achieve the result. For the very inhibited woman, proper stimulation may have to be employed for over an hour before the first orgasm takes place. If the wife begins to feel guilty, frightened, or impatient, and won't let her husband caress her, she may never receive sufficient stimulation to experience a climax.

Couples who are willing to experiment and to communicate with each other have an easier time overcoming problems. They can experiment by caressing different places to find out for themselves what is most stimulating. They can each tell the other what places to caress and how, until they become knowledgeable of the best means of arousing the other. The couple usually discover, for example, that quite vigorous manual stimulation or too heavy pressure applied to their sexual organs, particularly at the start of love play, may have a numbing effect rather than an arousing effect, whereas the same general type of caressing, but with a more delicate, deliberate touch, may have a most stimulating result. The point is, each couple have to learn where, how, and for how long to stimulate each other to achieve the desired result. Caressing in the wrong places, in the wrong manner, for an insufficient period of time will not achieve the wanted effect. More will be said in a later chapter of lovemaking techniques.

PSYCHOLOGICAL BLOCKS

Psychological blocks to sexual response may include any type of negative feelings: fear, anxiety, stress, depression, embarrassment, guilt, disgust, or hostility. These blocks prevent individuals from participating fully in a sexual experience, or prevent them from "letting themselves go" so they respond fully to each other. *Fear* is one of these negative feelings which can inhibit sexual response. Fear may be of pregnancy, of being hurt, of failure, of rejection or ridicule, or of discovery. In the following example, fear of impregnating his wife was great enough to cause temporary impotence in the husband.

> Mr. and Mrs. P. came in for counseling at the insistence of Mrs. P. The couple were in their middle forties and had a history of satisfying sexual relations ever since they had been first married twenty years ago. Then several months prior to the consultation, Mrs. P. was shocked to discover she was pregnant. She absolutely did not want another child, especially at her age, so went to her doctor, who aborted the baby in the sixth week of development. Mrs. P. was much relieved, but Mr. P. began to worry about his wife getting pregnant again. Every time he tried to have intercourse with her, he found he was impotent.

The above example illustrates the effect of fear on the erectile response of the husband. No husband can will an erection—that is, have an erection because he wants to. Erection is not under voluntary control. It's a completely involuntary response to physical and mental stimuli. In this case, the husband was afraid, subconsciously, of having intercourse for fear he would impregnate his wife again. This deep-seated fear was enough to prevent an adequate erection, thereby relieving the husband of the capacity of having intercourse. Some wives who fear pregnancy have difficulty in participating fully in sexual relations, so they unconsciously hold back, which may prevent them from enjoying intercourse or responding completely.

Fear of being hurt is quite common, especially in a new bride, or especially during pregnancy or after childbirth. The wife who is afraid that intercourse may harm her unborn child finds it difficult to relax enough or to give herself fully enough really to enjoy sex. Vaginismus, which is the involuntary contraction of the muscles of the vagina, is really a physical reaction to fear, so that penetration cannot take place. Fear of failure can also be a strong enough feeling to motivate a husband or a wife to avoid intercourse entirely. The husband who was impotent on one occasion, who becomes fearful of repeating the failure, may try to avoid sexual relations. Or the wife who was not able to have an orgasm becomes fearful that the same thing will happen again, so she begins finding excuses so she won't have to make love to her husband. One common reaction of both husbands and wives is to blame the other person for one's failure. The unmarried couple who park along a dark roadside to make love, but who are afraid of being caught in the act by the police or by a passing friend, may find their lovemaking to be completely futile. They can't relax enough to respond.

Anxiety about any number of things may be sufficient to block response. The mother who is worried about a sick child may not be able to concentrate on making love. The husband who is worried about unpaid bills, or about finding a job, may have the same trouble. One husband told of their problem.

My wife and I have a fantastic sexual life except when we have company sleeping over in the next room. Our bed is old and it squeaks something awful. We get along fine with our lovemaking until I get on top and start thrusting up and down too hard, then the bed begins squeaking so loud you can hear it all over the house. When that happens, forget it. My wife turns off like she jumped into a tub of ice cubes. It's no use after that. When we're alone though, it never happens. She gets excited and forgets all about everything.

Couples who live in cramped quarters where there is a lack of privacy may become very anxious about making noise and so be unable to enjoy sex. One wife used to like intercourse until her oldest teen-ager walked in on her and her husband when they were all undressed, without any covers on the bed, and just as they both were reaching a climax. For several months afterward, the wife had trouble relaxing, even after her husband put an inside lock on their bedroom door.

Various *emotional illnesses* may impair sexuality. When people are emotionally depressed, sex is the farthest thing from their minds. Men or women who are under chronic stress or fatigue may lose sexual motivation. It has been found, for example, that men under chronic stress show a consistent decline in the testosterone level in their blood. Since testosterone is the male hormone which stimulates sexuality, a decline in the level results in a diminishing of sexual interest and capacity.

Embarrassment may also be a strong deterrent to sexual response. Some people have been brought up to be overly modest about their bodies. Their parents never allowed anyone in the family to see anyone else nude (not even the baby). Toilet procedures always took place behind closed doors. Dressing and undressing was strictly private, with the sexes segregated. Children were punished for even handling their genitals. Anything that had to do with sex was considered dirty, so that any normal curiosity was suppressed. The children may have been overly protected while growing up, to be certain to keep contacts with the opposite sex quite minimal. Courting opportunities were either denied or closely supervised. As a result, such persons enter marriage feeling very ashamed or guilty about anything having to do with the body or with sex. If the children grow up feeling that "nice boys or girls don't think or talk about sex," they may find extreme difficulty adjusting to the intimacies of married life. There are husbands or wives who have never seen each other dressing or undressing, or nude, who have never had intercourse unless it was in complete darkness. Some of these persons are so inhibited that they won't go to a physican for assistance, won't read literature that could help, or won't talk about sex with each other, which could help even more. Until the couple are able to overcome part of their modesty and embarrassment, they will continue to have difficulty.

Guilt may be strong enough to block sexual response. Individuals who are taught that premarital and extramarital sex are wrong, but who violate their own ethical principles, may be so guilt-ridden that they subsequently have problems. One husband described having sexual relations with another woman while on a business trip to South America. The sexual encounter resulted in conception and the birth of an illegitimate child. The husband felt guilty and fearful that his wife would find out, so that he was impotent with her for a considerable period of time afterward.

NEGATIVE FEELINGS TOWARD ONE'S PARTNER

How one feels toward one's sexual partner is also important in influencing sexual response. Many a male has gone to a prostitute to have sex only to discover that he was so disgusted by the whole experience that he couldn't do anything anyhow. A sensitive wife who is disgusted by her husband's crude language or behavior may be turned off by his advances, as is the wife who can't stand her husband when he is drunk or smelling like a brewery. The fastidious husband or wife may be so disgusted by unpleasant odors, or by other evidences of lack of personal cleanliness, that making love under such circumstances becomes almost impossible.

Couples whose relationship to each other becomes hostile, angry, or resentful may find more and more difficulty responding to each other sexually. This is why it is difficult to separate one's sexual life from one's total relationship. What affects the total husband-wife relationship may also affect the couples' sexual life. It's hard to fight all day long and then make love willingly, freely, and completely that night. This is why couples who have love and respect in their relationship tend to be more responsive sexually than those who have disturbed relationships.

A minority of couples are able to separate sex from other aspects of their relationship, so that they can be quite hostile toward each other and still have sex together. In such cases, however, sex becomes just erotic response without any emotional feeling, or, if any feeling is there, it may be negative, so that sex becomes a means of expressing anger, hostility, or of inflicting punishment or pain on the other. Certainly, under these circumstances, it is not an expression of tender feelings of affection and love.

PHYSICAL CAUSES

Some problems have a physical origin. One most frequent cause of sexual problems is the taking of certain drugs, particularly drugs that have a sedative effect. *Alcohol* is probably the most common sedative. It may have a stimulating effect in small quantities, since its first effect is to release inhibitions that prevent response when the couple are sober. For this reason, some couples have sex only when they have been drinking. They find that alcohol relaxes them, minimizes anxieties, and makes them less inhibited. A wife who is very bashful or shy, for example, may really be able to "let herself go" sexually only after she has had a drink. The same is true of *marihuana,* which, like alcohol, is an intoxicant. It releases inhibitions, so that couples do things under its influence that they would never do ordinarily.

However, in quantity, alcohol's next effect is as a sedative that dulls sensations and blocks responses, so that complete participation is impossible. Consuming quantities of alcohol is one of the principal causes of impotence in males. Over a period of time, it may cause damage to the nerves that control erectile response. Such a condition is quite prevalent in chronic alcoholism. Recent research is suggesting also that smoking large quantities of marihuana over a period of time may reduce the male hormone, testosterone, found in the bloodstream. Whether this results in impotence in some males is a matter of dispute. There is some evidence that it may. It is known that mild doses may have a stimulating effect, especially on persons who tend to be sexually inhibited otherwise.

Similarly, small doses of sedatives such as *barbiturates* may release inhibitions temporarily, resulting in an increase in sexual appetite or response, but large doses act as depressants of sexual behavior and response. Chronic abuse of such sedatives diminishes human sexuality. Narcotics such as heroin or morphine act an analgesics, having a depressive effect on the central nervous system and on sexual response.

Stimulants such as *amphetamines,* taken in small doses, may enhance the sexual interest, performance, and abandonment of some persons. However, habitual use leads to a physical addiction, and to a decrease in sexual interest and performance. The "speed freak" is a severely addicted person who is usually very sick and psychotic and certainly not interested in sex.

There are numerous other drugs that affect sexual response. *Anticholinergic drugs,* which are used in treating peptic ulcers, glaucoma, or other eye disorders, inhibit the transmission of the nerve impulses that control erection and may therefore cause impotence. Similarly, *antiadrenergic drugs,* used in treating hypertension or vascular disorders, block nerve impulses and so may cause impotence or ejaculatory failure. *Sex hormones* may also affect sexuality. The female hormone *estrogen,* found in birth control pills, may over a period of time decrease sex desire in women, as will other hormones that exert an antiandrogenic effect. Thus, the steroids *cortisone* and *ACTH,* commonly used in treating allergies, may oppose the stimulating action of androgen on the brain and sexual organs. The best advice that can be given to the person who is having sexual problems and is on any type of medication is to find out if the drug that he or she is taking has an inhibiting effect on sexual interest and response. There are some drugs, such as tranquilizers like *Valium,* which are used to treat anxiety and as muscle relaxers, which may have no direct sexual effects in recommended doses but may indirectly increase sexual interest as the anxiety diminishes. Of course, when abused, these tranquilizers will inhibit sexual response patterns. Under all circumstances, persons ought to check with their physicians.

Numerous physical illnesses also affect one's sexual life. *Hepatitis* diminishes sexual interest. *Diabetes* may affect the erectile response of men. *Multiple sclerosis* may cause impotence or orgastic problems. Numerous *local diseases* of the female genitals may cause dyspareunia, or painful intercourse. *Severe malnutrition* or *vitamin deficiencies* in either males or females may affect arousal capacity and orgasm. *Heart* and *lung diseases* and various types of malignancies may decrease sexual desire and impair arousal capacity. In all cases of sexual problems that may be caused by ill-health, people should get expert medical advice to determine what needs to be done. In any type of sexual problem, physical factors ought to be checked out before emotional or psychological causes are suspected.

SUMMARY

Causes of Sexual Problems

Ignorance

> A lack of knowledge and understanding of sexual anatomy, sexual response, and lovemaking techniques.

Inadequate Stimulation

Lack of stimulation in the right places, in the right manner, and for a long enough period of time.

Psychological Blocks

Fear: of pregnancy, of being hurt, of failure, of rejection, of ridicule, of discovery.

Anxiety: about anything—a sick child, unpaid bills, unemployment, lack of privacy.

Emotional illness: stress or depression.

Embarrassment: excessive modesty in relation to the human body and sex; negative, repressive sex education while growing up.

Guilt: over a violation of one's ethical standards of sexual morality.

Negative Feelings Toward One's Partner

Disgust, hostility, anger, upset in the couple's relationship.

Physical Causes

Drugs

Physical illness

4

MEN, WOMEN, AND THEIR SEXUAL RESPONSE

IT has been mentioned that one of the reasons why couples have sexual problems is that they lack an understanding of the basic facts of human sexual anatomy, response, and love-making techniques. This chapter focuses on sexual anatomy and sexual response, and on some similarities and differences between men and women. The next chapter will discuss pleasuring and lovemaking techniques.

MALE AND FEMALE ANATOMY

Male Reproductive System. The diagram (p.49) shows the basic parts of the male reproductive system. Each of these parts performs an important function. The male sperm are produced in the pair of *testes* (enclosed in the sac, or *scrotum*) and stored in the *epididymis*. At the time of orgasm, the sperm are propelled up the *vas deferens,* are joined by a milky-white fluid—semen—from the *seminal vesicle* and an additional fluid from the *prostate gland,* and are ejaculated in spurts out the erect *penis.* At the time of climax, the testicles are pulled by muscles up closer to the body cavity to make ejaculation easier. At the same time, the opening to the *bladder* closes so the sperm do not enter, and thus urination is not possible at the same time that orgasm occurs. It is important to understand also that the center of sexual excitement in males is the penis, especially the bulbous end (the *glans*), so during love play this area should receive the pri-

MALE REPRODUCTIVE SYSTEM

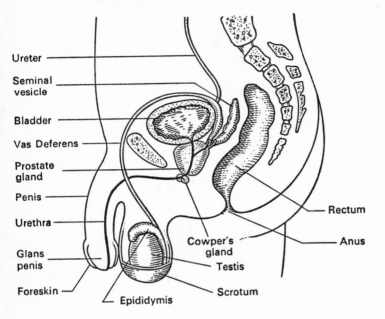

mary attention for maximum stimulation. Whether the male is circumcised (the *foreskin* removed) or uncircumcised (the skin intact) has no effect on sexual feeling, since at the time of a firm erection the foreskin is naturally pulled back away from the head of the penis anyhow. Also, the size of the penis has nothing to do with sexual capacity. Smaller penises tend to expand more in size when erect than do penises that are larger, so size differences are partially reduced. Furthermore, the smaller penis is just as sensitive as a larger one, so that there is no difference in pleasurable sensations. And since the woman's sexual feelings are located largely around the clitoris and the opening to the vagina, the husband with a smaller organ can give just as much pleasure as if his penis were larger.

The diagram also shows a pair of glands, the *Cowper's glands,* one located on each side of the *urethra.* Under sexual stimulation, the Cowper's glands secrete several drops of fluid which pass out of the penis prior to ejaculation. This serves as a lubricating fluid during intercourse. Since there may be some live sperm in the urethra, the passage of this fluid may carry sperm to the outside. Couples who have relied on withdrawal as the means of contraception may find that impregnation has occurred, and this is because sperm are deposited in the vagina when the fluid from the Cowper's glands is secreted. Thus, conscientious withdrawal prior to orgasm is already too late. This is why withdrawal is not recommended as a reliable means of birth control.

The testes serve another important function besides the production of sperm. They secrete the male hormone *testosterone,* which is responsible for the development and preservation of masculine secondary sexual characteristics, including facial and body hair, voice change, muscular and skeletal development, and for the development of the other male sex organs: the seminal vesicles, prostate gland, epididymis, penis, and scrotum. Males with an insufficiency of testosterone may have a low sexual drive, a low sperm count, or show feminine physical traits. So whenever a male has a low sexual drive, the level of testosterone in the blood should be checked to see if the cause is physical.

Perhaps a word should be added about a vasectomy as a means of birth control for the couples who already have all the children they want. Vasectomy is *not* castration (which is the removal of the testicles and which is never done as a means of contraception). Vasectomy involves cutting the vas deferens slightly above the testicles, and then tying or otherwise closing off the remaining ends. This prevents sperm from passing upward from the testicles. The male still ejaculates semen, but it contains no sperm. The testicles still produce testosterone, so the man has as much sexual feeling and drive as before. He still has all of his former masculine traits.

There are some men who fear that a vasectomy will interfere with their sexual life or masculinity. Such is not so. From a physical standpoint, nothing is different except that the *ejaculate* does not contain sperm. Only the man who cannot accept such an operation psychologically may have sexual problems, but because of his negative emotional reactions, anxieties, and fears, not because of any physical change. Obviously, the male who may have adverse feelings about such an operation ought not to have it done.

Female Reproductive System. The diagram (p. 53) shows the basic parts of the female reproductive system. The *ovaries* serve two functions: the production of mature egg cells and the secretion of the female hormones *estrogen* and *progesterone* on a cyclical basis during the monthly cycle. Estrogen stimulates the development of female sex characteristics, such as breast development, the growth of pubic hair, and the development of the mature female figure. Progesterone, which is secreted during each monthly cycle after *ovulation* (after the egg cell has been discharged), helps control the length of the menstrual cycle from ovulation until the next menstruation, prepares the uterus for possible pregnancy, and helps maintain a pregnancy itself. It is also important in keeping breast tissue firm and healthy, and in reducing the possibility of premenstrual tension and painful menstruation.

The ovaries cease to function after *menopause* takes place, but even though they atrophy and no longer produce egg cells or hormones, sexual drive and capacity in the female remains strong. In fact, most women maintain an active and pleasurable sexual life well into their seventies or beyond. It is obvious that two functioning ovaries are not necessary for sexual response, so that women who have had their ovaries removed because of disease, or who have gone through the menopause, maintain the same interest and ability to enjoy sex as before. One reason is that sexual drive in the woman is controlled partially by the level of the androgens, or *male hormones* in her bloodstream, in relation to her level of estrogen. Occasionally, women with a low sexual drive are given male hormones, but the doctor must be careful or the woman will also grow a mustache and body hair, develop masculine musculature and strength, an enlarged clitoris, and other masculine characteristics. Similarly, males with an excess of the female hormone estrogen may evidence decreased potency and sexual drive and an enlargement of the breasts. In other words, both men and women have both male and female hormones in their bloodstream, but it is their relative balance which determines male or female physical characteristics, and it is having a high enough level of male hormones or androgens which exerts the primary influence on sexual drive.

The center of sexual excitement in the female is the *clitoris,* the equivalent of the male penis. This small organ, lying just above the area where the inner lips *(labia minora)* come together, is mostly hidden within a sheath of skin. Occasionally, the tip is visible from the outside. It is a highly sensitive organ, and very responsive to either manual or penile stimulation. It becomes erect under sexual excitement.

The external female sexual organs are known collectively as the *vulva* and include the *mons pubis* (the mound of Venus), the *vestibule* (the cleft region enclosed by the labia minor), the *labia majora* (major, or outer, lips), the *labia minora,* and the *clitoris.* The *hymen* is the rim of tissue that partly closes the *vagina* of the virginal woman. The *Bartholin's glands,* located on each side of the vaginal orifice, secrete a drop or so of fluid during sexual excitement, making the walls of the vagina moist, and acting as lubricating fluid during intercourse. The total area of the vulva, including the labia, mons, and clitoris, is sensitive and ought to be stimulated during love play to achieve sexual excitement. Since the nerve endings in the vagina lie deep beneath the surface, very little feeling is aroused internally, until sexual excitement is already well advanced. Some women have almost complete vaginal anesthesia, so sexual arousal comes by clito-

FEMALE REPRODUCTIVE SYSTEM

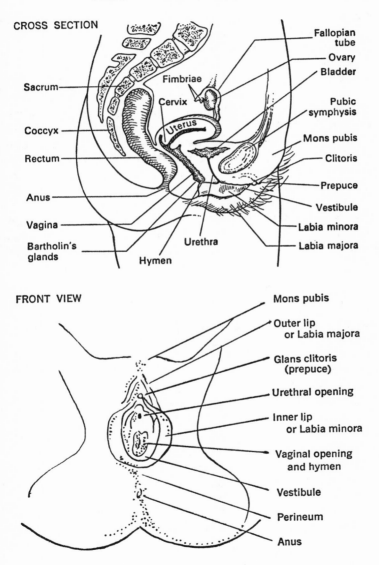

CROSS SECTION

Fallopian tube
Ovary
Bladder
Fimbriae
Sacrum
Cervix
Pubic symphysis
Coccyx
Uterus
Mons pubis
Rectum
Clitoris
Prepuce
Anus
Vestibule
Vagina
Labia minora
Bartholin's glands
Urethra
Labia majora
Hymen

FRONT VIEW

Mons pubis
Outer lip or Labia majora
Glans clitoris (prepuce)
Urethral opening
Inner lip or Labia minora
Vaginal opening and hymen
Vestibule
Perineum
Anus

ral rather than by vaginal stimulation. Usually during intercourse penile thrusting tugs on the labia, which in turn caresses the clitoris, resulting in sexual stimulation. In some cases, couples have to stimulate the clitoris manually during intercourse itself for the woman to achieve orgasm. These details will be discussed in Chapter 16.

It's important to recognize that there is no physiological difference between a so-called *vaginal orgasm* (achieved by vaginal stimulation) and a *clitoral orgasm* (achieved by clitoral stimulation). The physical response is the same, even though the method of stimulation is different. Most couples enjoy sex more through regular intercourse than by mutual masturbation, but usually because they are physically closer and more intimate during intercourse. There is greater emotional satisfaction in this close contact. But as far as physiological response is concerned, an even more intense reaction may be achieved by some couples by manual stimulation than by intercourse. Ideally, manual caressing plus intercourse achieves the pleasures and results of both types of stimulation.

THE PROCESS OF SEXUAL RESPONSE

Stages. Masters and Johnson have divided the process of human sexual response into four stages: the *excitement phase,* the *plateau phase,* the *orgasmic phase,* and the *resolution phase.* (Masters and Johnson, 1966) It is helpful if couples understand exactly what happens during these stages. The excitement phase extends from the beginnings of sexual stimulation until the individual reaches a high degree of sexual excitation. The duration of this phase may be prolonged or shortened, depending upon the intensity of the stimulation and individual reactions to it. Cessation of stimulation or the presence of objectionable psychological factors may even abort the process. If effective sexual stimulation is continued, sexual tensions are intensified and the individual reaches the second, or plateau, phase of the sexual cycle, from which he or she may move to orgasm. If sexual stimuli or the drive to culminate the activity in orgasm is inadequate and sexual stimuli are withdrawn, the individual will not achieve orgasm and sexual tension will gradually subside.

The orgasmic phase is limited to those few seconds during which sexual tension is at its maximum and then suddenly released. Women usually vary more in the intensity and duration of orgasm than do men. After orgasm, the person enters the last, or resolution, phase of the sexual cycle, during which sexual tension subsides as the individual moves back through the plateau and the excitement phases to return to the unstimulated state.

Physiological Responses. As sexual excitement increases, both men and women show similar physical responses:

Erection—The man's penis, the woman's clitoris, the nipples of the female breast (a majority of men also evidence nipple erection), and the woman's labia become engorged with blood, which causes swelling, enlargement, and erection.

Increase in heart and pulse rate, blood pressure, respiration, and perspiration—The heart, pulse, and respiratory rates may more than double; the blood pressure may increase anywhere from 20 to 80 percent. About a third of men and women evidence perspiration during the resolution phase.

Sex flush—There is a noticeable reddening of the skin of the body, usually in the form of red, splotchy rash, gradually spreading over more and more of the body as excitement increases. About 3 out of 4 women, and 1 out of 4 men, show this reaction.

Myotonia—Muscular tension of both voluntary and involuntary muscles. As excitement increases, there is a tensing and flexing of the muscles of the arms, legs, abdomen, face, neck, pelvis, buttocks, hands, and feet. During orgasm, there may be severe involuntary muscular contractions throughout the body, gradually subsiding during the resolution phase. These contractions during orgasm are especially strong in the vagina, uterus, and pelvic region of the female, and in the penis, vas deferens, seminal vesicles, and prostate gland of the male.

Other changes in the sex organs—One of the most important changes in the female is in the vagina. The outer one third becomes engorged with blood, reducing the opening, with the outer muscles contracting around the penis. At the same time, the vaginal length increases, and the inner portion balloons out, increasing considerably in width. Women who use diaphragms for contraception have to be certain they are quite tight-fitting, otherwise the ballooning out of the inner vagina under sexual excitement loosens the diaphragm, allowing sperm to pass around the edges or causing the diaphragm itself to become dislodged. Under sexual excitement, the uterus increases in size by 50 percent and pushes outward during the contractions of orgasm, expelling any fluids that may be inside. If orgasm is during the menstrual period, increased flow may result for a brief period of time.

The most important change in the penis is erection and increase in width and length. It is not uncommon for an erection to come and go several times if the excitement phase is prolonged. It is also affected by fear, anxiety, changes in temperature, loud noises, changes in lighting, or other distractions. The testes also enlarge by at least 50 percent because of engorgement with blood during sexual excitement.

There are two significant things that ought to be added about these physiological reactions under sexual excitement. Even though the male and female sexual organs are different, similar reactions occur: both men and women show vasocongestion of the sexual organs (engorgement with blood) when stimulated, both have erectile tissue, both show an increase in heart rate, pulse rate, blood pressure, respiration, and possibly perspiration. Both show sexual flush. Both show an increase in muscular tensions during excitement, and rhythmic contractions during orgasm.

The second significant point that ought to be added is that regardless of the method of stimulation—whether manually by masturbation, or by mutual love play, or by intercourse—the physiological reactions are the same. The only variation is in the depth and intensity of these reactions. These vary from person to person, and they vary at different times in the same person. The intensity of orgasm can vary with any method of stimulation, and depends upon numerous physical and psychological factors in the total situation.

MALE AND FEMALE DIFFERENCES

Orgasm Capacity. In spite of the similarities between men and women in the way they respond sexually, there are also some important differences. For one thing, women are much more capable of multiple orgasms than are men, and are more capable of prolonged orgasmic response. The graph (p. 58) shows the typical response of a female who has three orgasms. After the first orgasm, if sexual excitement is allowed to diminish briefly, and stimulation resumed, a second orgasm occurs, followed by a reduction in excitement to the plateau level. If at that point restimulation occurs again, the woman climaxes again. Some wives are capable of numerous orgasms (four or five are not unusual) under the right circumstances. In fact, some wives frequently desire multiple orgasms to be satisfied. The husband needs to follow his wife's lead and suggestions, and she should be willing to indicate to him her needs and desires. If the husband cannot sustain an erection while his wife has multiple orgasms, he can stimulate his wife manually after he loses his erection. The graph also shows the curve of the wife who is excited to the plateau phase but never has a climax at all. In this case, the resolution of feelings and bodily changes takes much longer.

There are a minority of men who are capable of two or, rarely, three orgasms if sufficient time elapses in between, but these are exceptions rather than the rule. Usually the

HUMAN SEXUAL RESPONSE CYCLES

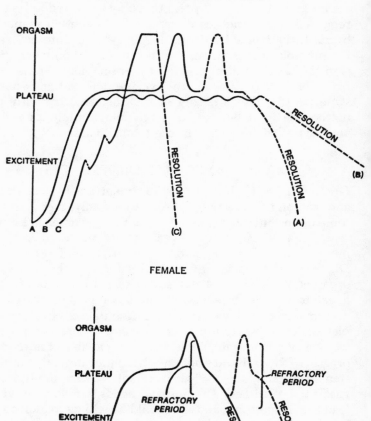

FEMALE

MALE

From W. H. Masters and V. E. Johnson, *Human Sexual Response* (Little, Brown & Co., 1966), p. 5. Copyright ©1966 by William H. Masters and Virginia E. Johnson. Reprinted by permission.

men are young. Abstinence from sexual experience during a number of days previous also increases the man's sexual capability.

Sexual pleasure does not, however, depend upon the number of orgasms but upon their intensity and the satisfaction derived from the total experience. One intense orgasm may be far more satisfying than several shallow ones. Usually, each succeeding orgasm after the first, in men, is less intense and pleasurable, whereas, in women, succeeding orgasms may be more intense and pleasurable than the first. Often, in women, the initial orgasm is only a prelude to a more intense orgasm which follows if stimulation continues.

Sources of Arousal. Men and women are also aroused differently. Kinsey and others observed that men were aroused by erotic pictures and stories, talking about sex, looking at women with shapely figures, observing sexual activity of humans or animals, or by looking at nude photos. (Kinsey, 1948) Women were not as much aroused by these sources as by reading love stories or seeing romantic movies. (Kinsey, 1953) Thus, men have always been considered *erotic* and women *romantic*.

However, more recent research findings indicate that when women were exposed to erotic photographs they reported them to be less arousing than did men, but when they were actually examined medically, the degree of physiological reactions of the women were almost the same as for the men. (Sigusch, 1970) It was obvious that society had taught the women that they were not supposed to be aroused by such sources, so they reported they were not, when in fact they were. Thus, social conditioning has had something to do with the way men and women respond sexually. However, most men and women are more responsive in romantic, loving settings, so psychological factors remain a strong component to sexual satisfaction.

Time. There seem to be some differences in the time required for orgasm to take place, depending upon the method of stimulation. If a couple copulate without prior love play, Kinsey found that the average male reached a climax in 4 minutes of intercourse and the average female required 10 to 20 minutes. But when properly stimulated through masturbatory and pleasuring techniques, the average woman was able to climax in less than 4 minutes (Kinsey, 1953): about the same length of time required for men. The reason it took longer in the first instance for the female to climax was that she was not properly stimulated before intercourse took place. Once the husband knows how to arouse his wife prior to actual intromission (when the penis enters the vagina), she is able to reach an orgasm quickly. This is important to remember if the husband tends to come too quickly, or if the wife has difficulty having an orgasm before her husband's erection subsides. Proper preparation and extended love play is one key to the orgasmic satisfaction of the wife.

Erogenous Zones. The bodily areas of sexual sensitivity, called *erogenous zones,* are also somewhat different in men and women. In females, these areas are more widespread and diffuse, whereas in males they are more localized around the genital area. Women find that their breasts, especially their nipples, are a highly sensitive area. In fact, most women prefer breast stimulation before genital stimulation commences, since they experience enhanced pleasure in this way. Most also respond more easily to the caressing of the clitoris, and to a lesser extent to stimulation of the mons pubis and the labia. Others also enjoy caressing of the inner thighs, the buttocks, the anus, shoulders, the small of the back, neck, or earlobes, although these areas are not as sexually sensitive as the genitals and the breasts. The tongue and the lips are also very sensitive. In fact, most women enjoy being caressed over the entire body, along with embracing and kissing. When several thousand married women were asked what types of physical expression gave them the greatest satisfaction, they indicated that the closeness or feeling of oneness with their partner was the most important, followed by orgasm itself. Coitus and foreplay (petting) ranked third and fourth in importance. (Bell and Bell, 1972) The fact that a woman's feelings are quite diffuse means that she requires a period of wooing, bodily contact, and love play before she is physically and emotionally ready for intercourse itself.

Since the most intense sexual feelings in men are concentrated in the genital area, and especially in the penis, these areas should receive the most attention if there is a need to increase sexual excitement rapidly. Most men also enjoy having the testicles, inner thighs, buttocks, anus, chest, abdomen, and the entire body carressed, although these activities may not be sexually arousing. The man's lips and tongue, like those of the woman, are highly sensitive to touch.

Age Differences. Age is also an important factor in sexual appetite and desires, and here too men and women show some differences. The graph (p. 62) shows the relative sexual drive versus age of males and females. As seen in the graph, men reach the peak of their sexual drive in their late teens and early twenties, whereas women reach the height of their drive in their late thirties or early forties. These are averages, of course, and individuals may differ from these norms. One interesting thing about the graph is that there is no physical reason why these differences should exist. In fact, since women become sexually mature earlier than men, it would seem more likely that their sexual drive would begin at a younger age than that of men. But it doesn't. Why so? The reason is in the differences in the way men and women are conditioned by our culture. Women have always been taught to inhibit their sexual feelings, men to express theirs. Thus, for some women, it may take years before they become completely sexually responsive with as strong a sexual appetite as their husbands. This is one reason why early marriages are often difficult: the young husband is at the height of his sexual drive; the wife's feelings are only beginning to become

SEXUAL DRIVE IN MALES AND FEMALES

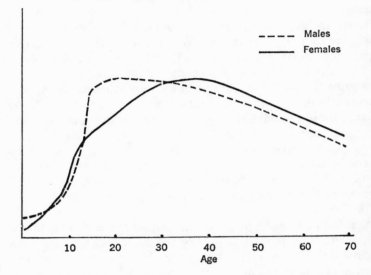

aroused and only slowly does she become responsive. This is also one reason for some sexual difficulties during the middle years. The wife's desires are at their peak; the husband's needs may already be tapering off. This is why many middle-aged wives are frustrated and complain that their husband is not as attentive as they desire.

Of course, modern females are not as often reared with such strong sexual inhibitions, so more and more young women show the same strong desire for sex as their husband. In fact, women today, even young women, are more often complaining that their husband doesn't satisfy them. This has created more marital conflicts and problems of male impotence in those cases where the wife is more demanding than the husband can satisfy.

Cyclical Desire. Another important difference between the male and the female is in the greater cyclical desire of women than men. Part of the woman's variations in sexual drive relate to the time of her monthly cycle. Overall, women have greater sexual drive just before and after menstruation than at other times of the month. Some women report increased desire at the time of ovulation, but these women are in the minority. Of course, many factors affect desire: general health, the degree of marital harmony, events that happen in and outside the family, even current events. Whatever is upsetting may influence sexual drive and desire.

Men are affected by these events as well as women. A man who is in temporary ill-health, tired and exhausted, or is upset by his relationship with his wife or children, or by events at work, or in the world, may evidence a temporary decrease in sexual drive. But usually, male desire is more constant and less variable. Certainly, there is no male counterpart to the female fluctuations during different times of the menstrual cycle. However, male sexual drive is affected by the testosterone level. Fatigue may lower that level, and in most men the level is highest in the morning and lowest at night. This is one reason that many men show greater interest in intercourse in the morning than when they are tired at night. Emotional factors may play a role in influencing sexual desire in both men and women, but overall it is felt that women are more affected by them than men. Perhaps, here too, this is because of differences in the way men and women are brought up. In our culture, women are encouraged to express their feelings and emotions, men to inhibit them.

Individual Differences. The important thing to remember is that everyone—male or female—is an individual. Each person is different, is stimulated and responds in his or her own way, and so cannot be unfairly compared to anyone else. The important thing is that the husband and the wife—as individuals—are each happy and satisfied with their sexual life, and that together they are able to fulfill each other completely. In sex, as in other areas of married life, there is the temptation to try to keep up with the Joneses, to do what others are doing, or to measure one's relationship by that of others. Such efforts are a mistake. A couple ought to measure their sexual life by their mutual standards and desires, and to learn to please each other, not some fictitious couple by the name of Jones who live next door.

5

PLEASURING AND
LOVEMAKING TECHNIQUES

MOST married people would hesitate to confess: "I don't know how to make love." But the fact remains that thousands of people don't know how. Many of these persons are newly-weds and haven't had the benefit of years of practice and experience. But a goodly number have been married for a number of years. They just never really learned.

At the outset it must be emphasized that there is no right way and no wrong way to make love. Here again, the standard should not be what one reads in a marriage manual, or what someone else does, but the mutual feelings of the couple themselves: what they desire, want, and enjoy. Nevertheless, there are some basic principles, and some suggestions that are offered by sex therapists to couples who are having difficulties. These principles and techniques have proved highly effective and ought to be more widely known, but it must be realized that each couple will add their own ideas to make their lovemaking suit them.

PLEASURING

Instructions. Sex therapists talk about what is variously called "pleasuring" or "sensate focus" techniques. (Kaplan, 1974; Masters and Johnson, 1970) These techniques are especially helpful in overcoming problems of impotence, ejaculatory incompetence, frigidity, or orgasm dysfunction. But they are also helpful as a means of improving sexual satisfaction and pleasure.

Briefly, in learning to "pleasure" each other, husbands and wives are given the following instructions, or similar ones:

Get ready for bed by undressing and showering in a relaxed, unhurried way. Then get on your bed, nude, without covers, and with the light on if it is nighttime. Your first task is to learn to caress each other over many parts of the body, to learn how to give pleasurable feeling without the demand for orgasm, and to learn to communicate to each other the types of caresses that feel especially good to you. You may begin first with you (the husband) caressing your wife in many places other than her breasts and genitals. You (the wife) should first lie on your stomach so that your husband can caress the back parts of your body as gently and sensitively as he can. Then you (the husband) begin at the back of her neck, caressing her ears, shoulders, and back, working down to her buttocks, legs, and feet. Use your hands, and/or lips, if you desire, moving slowly and easily, striving to create as much pleasurable feeling as possible.

In the meantime, you (the wife) concentrate on what is happening, on the sensations you are feeling, trying not to let your mind wander or to think of other things. Let yourself feel everything, and then tell your husband what feels good and what does not, talking only enough to give guidance and suggestions. Tell your husband where you want to be touched, and how lightly or heavily, and whether to go slower or faster.

When you have had enough, you (the wife) then lie on your back so your husband can do the same thing with the front of your body. Initially though, don't (addressed to the husband) touch your wife's breasts, labia, vagina, or clitoris. Learn how to caress other parts first so your wife can learn what gives her the most pleasure, yet without the demand for sexual response, orgasm, or performance.

After this, it's your turn (addressed to the husband) to receive, and for your wife to pleasure you.

When pleasuring is used as therapy, it's important initially that couples avoid touching the genital areas or the wife's breasts. The initial goal is to learn how to give and receive pleasure apart from more direct sexual stimulation to orgasm.

When couples are able to give and receive this type of pleasure, freely and responsively, they are then instructed to include light, nondemanding stimulation of the genitals in their caressing. When this is used as treatment, initially, couples are instructed to cease the caressing *before* orgasm takes place. This way, the husband and the wife do not feel pressured to respond in a certain way, or to "perform" sexually in response to the other's demands. With the pressure to perform removed, it is easier for the impotent husband to become potent, or for the inorgasmic wife to become orgasmic. Under most circumstances, gentle, teasing, nondemand stimulation is a highly erotic experience, but only gradually as inhibitions are broken down, negative feelings overcome, and problems solved are couples able to proceed to full copulation and orgasm.

Purposes. The purpose of sensate focus therapy is to help couples get "in touch" with their previously avoided sensual and erotic feelings, to become sensitized to erotic wishes and caresses, and to learn to be free to give and experience sexual pleasure. Couples learn to talk about their feelings, needs, and desires, to communicate through words and touch, and to become sensitive to each other's desires and feelings. They are encouraged to use fantasy during the process, to entertain erotic thoughts, and to use their imagination in conjuring up sexual images which help them to respond. They learn to become receptive to many types of physical caresses, to overcome embarrassment and inhibitions, and to accept their sexuality and that of their mate in a nonjudgmental way, without shame or guilt, so they can fully enjoy the pleasure of loving sex with each other.

USING THESE PRINCIPLES
TO ENHANCE LOVEMAKING

Love Play. The principles of pleasuring, as described, are prescribed by therapists for couples who are having sexual difficulties. The use and application of these principles in the treatment of specific sexual problems such as impotence or orgasm dysfunction will be described in detail under the chapters dealing with specific problems. But, actually, the principles of pleasuring are sound and useful in assisting all couples who want to improve their sexual techniques and to enhance their experiences together.

The most satisfying lovemaking requires a period of love play, caressing, fondling, "pleasuring," before intercourse itself. The only real difference between using pleasuring as therapy and as part of lovemaking is the fact that in lovemaking, pleasuring ultimately culminates in coitus and orgasm. In therapy, at least in its initial stages, orgasm is deferred until orgasm can take place without threat of difficulty.

The first task of every couple is for the husband and the wife to learn how to caress each other throughout all parts of the body, to learn to communicate what feels good and what does not, and to learn to respond to the suggestions of the other. The following suggestions are offered which should facilitate the accomplishment of these objectives.

Lightly and Slowly. *Learn to use light touches, beginning the caressing in less sensitive areas and only gradually including the more sensitive areas.* Exceptionally gentle caressing gradually awakens the nerve ends of the genital region so that finger stroking of the abdomen, the inner thighs, or the woman's breasts prepares the partners for more direct stimulation of the genitals. The husband can gently massage the breasts, lightly brushing the nipple, occasionally tweaking it or rubbing it between his fingers, while his wife caresses his chest, inner thighs, or buttocks. Caressing with the hands interspersed with a light brushing with the tongue, alternated with soft kisses and sucking, helps to increase pleasure. The husband may even suck on one nipple and lightly caress the other with one hand while caressing the genitals with the other, while his wife caresses his penis and thighs with her hands.

Kissing of the mouth ordinarily precedes kissing of the others parts of the body, but it should be as varied as other caresses: with open mouth, closed mouth, light lip pressure, heavy pressure, tongue over lips, tongue between lips and inside the other's mouth. Deep, erotic kissing can be almost as sexually stimulating as direct genital stimulation.

The couple's hands should be constantly busy: darting, sliding, stroking, squeezing, massaging each other's body. As excitement builds, more and more attention can be devoted to the woman's clitoris and labia and to the man's penis. Love play may also continue almost to the point of orgasm before coitus begins, especially if one or the other has difficulty achieving an orgasm.

With Privacy. *Make love with privacy assured:* behind a locked door with the possibility of interruption at a minimum. Some couples are able to relax completely only when they are alone in the house. One wife remarked:

> I can't seem to relax when the children are home. I'm on edge, afraid they'll hear us, or that they will call me right in the middle of things, or that they will knock at the bedroom door. Since my husband doesn't have to go to work until long after the children are in school, we wait until then to make love. That way, we are able to really let ourselves go and enjoy it.

Couples who are never alone, who never have privacy because of a small house, trailer, or apartment, may have to go out of the house to make love. One couple have their station wagon equipped with an air mattress and sleeping bag. They drive to an isolated place to do their lovemaking. Others couples have to wait until late at night until everyone else is asleep, or wake up early before others are awake. Others soundproof their bedroom. Whatever is necessary and possible to do ought to be done if lovemaking is to be the kind of enjoyable, uninhibited experience it ought to be.

Naked. *Learn to make love completely in the nude, and with the lights on (if at night) or in the daytime so that you can see each other.* Most couples become sexually aroused through visual as well as through tactile stimulation. Also, being able to see what one is doing makes it easier to follow or give directions. One husband complained:

> My wife only wants to make love at night in complete darkness. When she knows we are going to have sex, she puts on her nightie with the high neck, sometimes even her sweater. Once, she even wore her bathrobe and fur coat on top of that. How can I get her worked up if I can't even touch her? She says I ought to make her want to make love. But when I try to touch her, she says I'm too clumsy. Who wouldn't be? I can't even get to her underneath all those clothes.

In this example, the wife put up as many defenses as possible to try to discourage her husband, since she was really not interested in sex. In ordinary circumstances, couples are embarrassed at the beginning of marriage and only gradually learn to overcome inhibitions. But being willing to make love while completely undressed facilitates pleasuring and adds to the total excitement of the experience. Most couples enjoy undressing each other, and certainly most men enjoy seeing their wives naked. One husband commented: "When I see my wife's breasts or pubic hair, I get turned on right away." Many wives are surprised also to discover that seeing their husband's erect penis is highly erotic and stimulating.

Unhurried. *Allow plenty of time to make love:* when there is sufficient time for preliminary love play and pleasuring, without the pressures of schedules and appointments, and without the demands of unfinished tasks. At times, couples feel like lying in bed all morning, or even all day, resting, eating, and making love. On other ocassions a half hour is satisfying to both. But all couples find that lovemaking is enhanced by an unhurried atmosphere—before and after climax—so that sexual expression can become a fine art, not a perfunctory experience.

Of course, the best-laid plans don't work out. The telephone or the doorbell rings, the baby cries, it starts to rain in through the open windows. All sorts of things or people interrupt. But couples can at least try to avoid such interruptions.

Time for Adjustments. *Recognize that sexual adjustments take time.* Some couples are able to make a satisfying sexual adjustment early in marriage. Others are never able to work things out. But for most couples, an intermediate period of time is required, perhaps several weeks or months. One study of married college women showed that approximately half the wives experienced orgasm within the first month of marriage, one fourth within the first year of marriage, and the other fourth took one or more years, or had never experienced it. (Landis and Landis, 1973) There may be psychological (emotional), physical, or social (environmental) blocks at the beginning of marriage which must be overcome before success is achieved. This takes time, so a couple shouldn't be surprised if it takes them days, weeks, or even months before they are as uninhibited as they need to be, know how to stimulate and please each other, before they have worked out their own frequency pattern, or before their mutual timing in intercourse is satisfactory. (They don't have to "come" together to have a satisfactory sexual life.)

Try. *Be willing to try and to learn.* One of the most important requirements for success is a willingness to try and to learn. Sometimes after a few failures, or unsatisfying attempts at intercourse and climax, couples feel they have failed. Such is not true. It is not uncommon for intercourse to be frustrating in the first days or weeks of marriage. The husband comes too fast, or the wife doesn't come at all, or intercourse is painful, or the husband loses his erection because he ejaculates prematurely, or he can't even get an erection, or the wife can't come through intercourse but only by hand. Sometimes the husband or the wife don't really try to work out differences. They just avoid each other. Or they continue mutual masturbation because they are used to it, can come more easily that way, and don't have to worry about contraceptives. But since a mutually satisfying adjustment is vital to many years of happy marriage, it is important for both the husband and the wife to be motivated to learn. If they can't succeed by themselves, they should read all they can, and get qualified help if needed.

Be Uninhibited. One of the uncertainties in the beginning is how uninhibited to be, but *couples need to learn to let themselves go completely, to be as completely uninhibited as possible consistent with their mutual feelings and desires.* They ought to avoid deliberately shocking or doing things that disgust the other. But they can gradually let themselves go as they become more and more aware of the acceptance of the other person.

Couples ought to feel free to use the mouth and the tongue as instruments of stimulation, touching various erogenous zones orally as well as with the fingers, hand, or genitals. However, methods of stimulation that they find objectionable ought not to be used. Lovemaking requires consideration for the feelings of the other person. There are no set rules: they ought to let their lovemaking lead them to do things that are acceptable to them both. Usually, the longer two people are married, the more uninhibited they become. It goes without saying that keeping all parts of the body scrupulously clean by daily washing and bathing is an absolute requirement for uninhibited lovemaking. The genital regions especially need daily washing, and just prior to lovemaking, since unpleasant odors build up only a few hours after a bath. James McCary in his book *Human Sexuality* writes:

> A man who is overweight, chronically unshaven, and slovenly dressed, and whose breath reeks of tobacco or alcohol, can hardly expect to be considered a desirable bed partner. . . . Similarly, a woman who looks better with cosmetics, but neglects to make up her face, sits around home in bathrobe and curlers, allows herself to become significantly overweight or underweight, permits even faint urine, vaginal, or underarm odors to emanate, or does not often shave her legs and underarms is setting the stage for loss of respect, admiration, and even love. . . .
>
> Certainly, before joining each other in bed . . . each partner should see to it that he (or she) has at least a clean body, fresh breath, and neat, attractive night clothes. To do otherwise is to neglect some of the most basic ingredients of a happy sex life. (McCary, 1973, p. 149)

Experiment. *Feel free to experiment with a variety of positions in intercourse.* They ought not to be limited to the so-called "missionary position"—face-to-face, with the man on top. Many wives find it easier to have an orgasm with themselves on top. They can move about more freely, and the angle of the penis is such that it is rubbing the clitoris more directly than when the husband is on top. With the wife below, especially if her knees are flexed and legs raised toward her abdomen, and especially if the husband is positioned fairly far down (toward the wife's feet), the penis may enter the vagina at such an angle that it does not touch or rub the clitoral area at all. In such a position, the wife may have difficulty in reaching an orgasm, whereas if she keep her legs stretched out straight, and the husband scoots up on her body as far as possible with his penis still inserted, the shaft of the penis is pushed against the vestibule and clitoral shaft, thus enhancing the wife's stimulation and the possibility of orgasm.

A pioneer in treating sexual problems, Dr. Abraham Stone, found that women differ in the distances between the vaginal opening and the clitoris. In some women, the distance is so great that the penis, at whatever angle, does not rub the clitoris sufficiently during intercourse to stimulate it. In these instances it may be necessary for the wife or the husband to rub her clitoris manually during intercourse to achieve orgasm. This is difficult for the husband to do while on top, but if his wife is above him, or if they are in various side-by-side positions, it is accomplished easily. Of course, couples may use several positions during lovemaking. One couple makes love with the wife on top until she has an orgasm, then they switch, with the husband on top until he climaxes. A wife may want to try sitting on top of her husband, who is seated on a chair. A husband may want to experiment with a rear entry. Whatever is pleasurable and acceptable to them both might be considered all right.

Physical Surroundings. *Physical surroundings may play a role in enhancing or retarding lovemaking.* Some couples can make love freely in their own bedroom, but are inhibited in someone else's house, in a motel, or in an automobile. Certainly a hard floor, or the bare ground (perhaps covered with stones and insects), is not conducive to lovemaking. Physical comfort is important, as is the immediate physical environment. Some couples learn to respond only when the lights are low or they are playing "our favorite song." The trouble with such conditioning is that when conditions aren't exactly right, response becomes impossible. They would do better to learn to respond under a variety of conditions. One husband complained:

My wife wants the television on while we're having intercourse. She says the children won't hear us. But I find it very distracting. Who wants to try to make out during the middle of *Police Story?* Every time I hear a gun shot or a siren, I can't even remember what I am supposed to be doing.

In an extreme example, one husband would not turn off the Sunday afternoon football game during intercourse. He kept watching the teams while making love. He still reached a climax, but his wife couldn't. In fact, she was disgusted and hurt by the whole experience. "He acts like he's more interested in football than he is in me."

Mutual Experience. *Lovemaking should be a cooperative, mutual experience.* Certainly, the wife ought to feel as free to initiate intercourse as the husband. Why shouldn't she indicate to him by word and behavior that she feels like making love? Similarly, she should caress her husband at the same time he is caressing her, so that love play becomes a mutually engaging experience occupying the full attention of both the husband and the wife. One husband complained:

My wife doesn't refuse me, but neither does she help much. She won't play with me at all, or really participate. She lies there like a bump on a log, never even moving.

It is much more satisfying to two persons for both of them to be loved and caressed, and it is more exciting for the wife as well as the husband to engage in pelvic thrusting and other movements that enhance the other person's pleasure as well as one's own. One husband bragged:

My wife is a superb lover. She knows how to rub me in all the right places with just the proper touch. She can move her hips and even her vaginal muscles inside so that she caresses my penis until it drives me wild. One night she asked me just to lie still and let her do all the work. What a night! It was beautiful. She said it was a marvelous experience for her too.

Traditionally, in our culture men have been taught to be the sexual aggressors and women passive recipients. As a result, some women are afraid to be too aggressive; they fear their husbands will think them unladylike. However, many husbands complain that their wives never take the initiative. "I'm always the one who has to start," one husband complained. Of course, a man or a woman can be too aggressive, constantly demanding, never really considering the other person. Such approaches create resentment. But to want intercourse and to be afraid to indicate one's desires to one's mate is also quite frustrating. Ideally, couples ought to be able to be honest enough, and accepting enough, to express their wishes and to be able to abide by each other's wishes whenever humanly possible. A husband or a wife who is repeatedly rejecting creates real barriers. The other person, not wanting to be rejected, withdraws and alienation and separation begin. Over a period of time, such a situation may wreck the marriage.

6

PSYCHOLOGICAL BLOCKS TO SEXUAL RESPONSE

IN Chapter 3 it was emphasized that psychological blocks to sexual response may include any type of negative feelings: shame, embarrassment, disgust, guilt, fear, anxiety, stress, depression, or hostility which prevents individuals from "letting themselves go" so they can respond fully to each other. This chapter discusses these psychological barriers more in detail, along with some suggestions for overcoming them.

SHAME, EMBARRASSMENT, DISGUST, AND GUILT

Negative Feelings About Sex

Paul C. was brought up in a family that belonged to a strict religious sect. This sect emphasized the sinfulness of the world and the need to separate oneself from it. Good Christians should not talk to those outside the sect, they should not participate in public school or community functions, they did not drive cars, go to parties, movies, or dances, or drink spirits, or smoke. They did not play cards, baseball, or engage in other sports. They did not wear fancy clothes or jewelry; the men did not shave their faces nor the women cut their hair. Any thoughts about sex or interest in it were especially sinful and were born of the devil. Any violation of the strict rules of the sect and one would burn in hell throughout all eternity.

When Paul was thirty-five years old, he came to our Twenties-n-Thirties (T.N.T.s) group at the church and began to participate in all the social events, including picnics and dances. But not without terrible guilt. He wanted to be in with the others, and did join us, but was very nervous, sweated profusely, and had terrible nightmares. He related how he would see the sunset in the evening with its brilliant crimson colors, but all he could think of were the fires of hell.

After almost a year of counseling and of regular attendance at T.N.T.s, Paul began to become more relaxed about wanting friendships and about entering into the fun of the group. He started dating a girl whom he liked—something he had never done before. But no matter how hard he tried, he could not overcome his strong feelings that any sexual urges or feelings were sinful. If he ever dared think about sex, he immediately repressed such thoughts. He realized that he would probably never marry, because he was sure he would never be able to make love to his wife. He had come a long way in his adjustment, but still faced a deep barrier of shame and guilt which had been built within his conscience. Paul's case is an extreme one, but is offered to show the disastrous effect of a completely negative and repressive upbringing on social and sexual adjustment.

In their efforts to prevent their children from being sexually promiscuous, or especially in trying to prevent their daughters from "getting into trouble," some parents unwittingly make it harder for their children to achieve mature and loving sexual adjustment once married. One teen-age girl remarked:

> Every time I go out the door my mother says to me: "Now don't get into trouble, don't let anything bad happen to you." After several weeks of this I asked her: "Exactly what do you mean, Mother?" and she replied: "I mean, don't let any boy touch you."

One can sympathize with this mother's feelings, but without realizing it, in trying to "keep her daughter out of trouble" she was also making it harder for her to relate to any man in a warm, loving way. Another mother told her daughter over and over again: "All men are lechers and filthy-minded. All they are interested in is one thing." As a result of this mother's teaching, this daughter never dated throughout high school; she dressed in "granny dresses," wore gold-rimmed glasses, braided her hair, wore shawls and "hippie style" beads and clothes. Only when she went away to college was she able to get out from under her mother's influence, begin to date and make normal heterosexual adjustments.

The effects of negative, repressive sex education vary from person to person, but they *may* result in any of the common problems of sexual dysfunction: sexual frigidity (in either men or women), impotence, orgasm incapacity in females or ejaculatory incompetence in men, dyspareunia, or vaginismus. Fortunately, most persons, given time, and sometimes therapeutic assistance, are able to overcome the effects of quite repressive upbringing. But overall, about 10 percent of American wives remain inorgastic. The major causes are negative conditioning.

Years ago the negative teachings of some religious groups concerning sex contributed to sexual difficulties. The latest research today, however, shows that those who are most religious are also more sexually well adjusted in marriage. The replies of 100,000 women in a *Redbook* survey revealed the following:

Women who described themselves as "strongly religious" were more likely to be satisfied with their sex lives than women who described themselves as "fairly religious" or "mildly religious." Strongly religious wives were most likely to describe their marital sex as "very good."

After age 25, strongly religious women were more sexually responsive than nonreligious women, that is, they were more likely to be orgasmic almost every time they engaged in intercourse.

Strongly religious and nonreligious wives of any one age

group engaged in intercourse with about the same frequency, but nonreligious wives more often expressed dissatisfaction with the frequency with which they had intercourse. This tendency was especially noticeable among women 25 to 34 years of age. One in three strongly religious wives and 1 in 2 of nonreligious wives said that sex occurred too infrequently.

Strongly religious wives were more likely to discuss their sexual feelings and desires with their husbands than were the nonreligious wives.

Strongly religious wives, no matter what age, were more likely than nonreligious wives to report that they always took an active part in lovemaking. (Levin and Levin, 1975)

One might ask: What is the reason for these differences between religious and nonreligious wives? One explanation is the fact that over the last twenty years more enlightened clergy have urged their churches to come to grips with the dilemmas of human sexuality, with the result that the churches have now been linking sex in a positive way with marital fulfillment, emphasizing that sexual pleasure is not only a legitimate expectation but also a necessary element in a good marriage. The churches are now teaching that sex not only is necessary for procreation but should also be used in marriage as a profound expression of love. A 1977 volume just issued by the Paulist Press, entitled *Human Sexuality, New Directions in American Catholic Thought,* says that "Christians must be encouraged to embrace their sexuality joyfully and in full consciousness." This same book even goes on to say that "no physical expression of sexuality, including oral sex, provided it be mutually sensitive and acceptable, should be judged as morally wrong or perverse." (The Catholic Theological Society of America, 1977) This attitude is a drastic change from the negative teachings of the churches of a generation ago.

Developing Positive Feelings. One way to overcome negative feelings about sex is to accept it for what it is: a God-given way of expressing the deepest love of which two human beings are capable. Sex can be dirty, tawdry, disgusting, but it can also be clean, enriching, sanctifying, and beautiful. It is neither moral nor immoral in and of itself, it depends upon how it is used. It can be used to hurt, to punish, as an expression of anger, hostility, or contempt. It can say to someone else: "I hate you. I want to hurt you. I have no regard for you." Or it can say: "I love you. I want to bring you joy, happiness, and fulfillment. I respect, adore, and treasure you." In this positive context, how can anyone say that sex is ungodly? There is need, therefore, to affirm our sexuality, to say to our mate: "I love you, and I want to express joyous, wonderful, exciting, pleasurable sex with you."

Some honest and deep-thinking persons believe that one way of eliminating sexual problems is through greater permissiveness, especially before marriage. Their reasoning is as follows. Repression of sex can cause problems; therefore, eliminate these problems by eliminating all repression. Make it possible for young people to express sex premaritally without guilt or fear of pregnancy and there won't be so many problems of sexual adjustment once married. I disagree completely with this line of thinking. Research studies have never proved that premarital sexual permissiveness is the way to avoid sexual hang-ups in young people. The young person who "sleeps around," without deep feeling, or without real involvement or commitment, learns that sex is meaningless, without feeling or emotion except physical pleasure. It can be engaged in at any time with anyone, but one does not have to be in love, or even to care about the other person. Sex is like eating a meal with people one does not know: there is no companionship or feelings for the others who are present.

This type of meaningless sex doesn't solve problems. It creates them. We are finding that more and more college students have been having sex without affection, but we are also finding that many of these students feel empty, ashamed of themselves, disgusted and disillusioned with sex, and become quite cynical about the opposite sex. There is growing evidence also that this is a contributing factor in the increasing incidence of impotence in college males. Because sex has no meaning, because there is no love involved, these males are being negatively conditioned. After a while, they are unable to respond at all. Sex without feeling is creating problems of sexual response for some persons.

What is the answer? Positive, truthful sex education of our children and adolescents, and greater encouragement of meaningful, loving sex, rather than permissive sex. Young people who are taught that the only Christian expression of sex is as an expression of love, in the context of a caring, committed, responsible relationship, are being encouraged not only to be responsive but also to make sex truly meaningful and fulfilling. Those youths who are encouraged to be permissive are being taught that sex is without real meaning, or feeling, and that its only function is to provide physical sensation. In the long run, this type of teaching is self-defeating and destructive of real humanity.

Negative and Positive Feelings About the Body. Attitudes about one's own body or other bodies also influence sexual responsiveness and adjustments. Most persons, while growing up, develop some feelings of modesty. But modesty can be a helpful thing or a harmful thing. A few girls still are brought up with such a sense of modesty that their honeymoon becomes a traumatic experience. They are fearful of the thought of taking off their clothes, of appearing disrobed in front of their husbands, of being touched, or of touching their husbands. One young girl who had seen a picture of a naked man in *Playgirl* remarked: "I'm never going to look at my husband's penis. I think they're ugly." Another girl was told by her girl friend that men sometimes put their fingers in a girl's vagina when they make love. She came home and asked her mother: "Is that what married people do? If that's so, I'm never going to get married."

Most women hate to go to the doctor for a Pap smear or

for a vaginal examination. The position in which they are placed for the examination is ludicrous and humiliating. But some wives have such extreme feelings that even when pregnant, they put off going to the doctor to get prenatal care. Since adequate care is quite crucial, especially in the early months of pregnancy, their excessive modesty can actually be very harmful to them and to their unborn baby.

At the opposite extreme, of course, are women or men who are exhibitionists, who enjoy flaunting their sexuality, who enjoy parading in swimsuits so skimpy that they leave almost nothing unexposed. As in most things, there is need here for moderation. Nudity, in and of itself, is not an evil. The Bible admonishes modesty as a way of avoiding temptation and a way of showing humility before God. Modesty serves useful functions. But there is nothing repressive about the way the Scriptures talk about human sexuality or the human body. The Song of Solomon is a poem of love, including love of the bodily form. A beautiful body is looked upon as an object of adoration and love.

One might object: "This is all right if you have a nice figure, or if you're under twenty-five. But most people over this age are too fat, with too many bulges in the wrong places, or, if they're old, they're wrinkled and saggy. Who wants to look at them?"

The answer is: Most husbands and wives have an erotic interest in each other's body, even if they no longer have an aesthetic interest. If one is fortunate enough to have a beautiful body, one's mate may enjoy looking at it just because it is so beautiful. If it is not beautiful, it can still be erotically interesting. A man or a woman who is considerably overweight is not beautiful by the standards of our culture. But the wife of one considerably overweight "tub of lard" (as she called him) remarked: "My husband may not have a beautiful body, but he has a magnificent penis. It gives me a lot of pleasure, and I love it, and him."

The purpose of this quote is not to shock (it is an honest observation), but to indicate that when two people love each other, they are able to accept each other as they are, and they usually find some physical features which they consider beautiful. Those features need not be exposed to the general public, but they are looked upon by their mates as objects of admiration. Will the wife who is flat-chested be afraid ever to undress in front of her husband? If so, she may deprive him of observing other of her body parts which he finds exciting.

It is helpful to marriage if couples develop a very casual attitude about nudity. By all means, they should expose themselves to each other. And, even if they start their love-making fully clothed, it is a lot easier to pleasure each other if they at least end up fully naked.

The same casualness about nudity should exist in the home as children are growing up. It *is* all right, and even helpful, to let small children see each other, and you, naked. A casualness about toileting and other bodily functions develops very accepting, matter-of-fact attitudes. Then, as children grow older, and they begin to want privacy, they should have it, in just as casual and matter-of-fact ways. As they reach puberty, they should be taught to dress modestly, not because they are ashamed of their bodies, but because these are the standards of our culture, and others will disapprove and get wrong impressions of their character if they don't. Also, daughters especially need to understand that if they dress provocatively, they will be sexually stimulating to boys, and this can cause problems for them as well as embarrassment for the boys. Consideration for themselves and others requires some common sense about dress. But it is hoped they will be encouraged to enjoy nudity thoroughly after marriage as an honest expression of loving, erotic interest in each other. In fact, it is helpful if newlyweds learn to feel comfortable while completely naked—working, eating, loving —within the privacy of their own home. Accepting nudity helps them to accept each other completely, as well as to free them to become sexually responsive.

Shame and Guilt About Touching the Body. Some children are brought up to feel that touching the genitals, or playing with them, is wrong and dirty. A baby boy innocently holds his penis, father slaps his hand and shouts: "Don't do that, it's dirty." A baby girl scratches her itchy vagina. Her mother pulls her hand away and warns: "Nice girls don't do that." In this way, and through other negative teaching, parents let children know that it is wrong to touch their genitals. These negative teachings sometimes carry over into adolescence and adulthood. When a group of high school boys and girls of a Congregational Church fellowship were asked to express their feelings about masturbation, three fourths of them said it was an unhealthy habit and detrimental to later sexual life; 1 out of 8 said it could be tolerated; only 1 out of 8 said there was nothing wrong with it. These youths were from a denomination that had no specific teaching against masturbation, yet still reflected the widespread prohibitions against masturbation that exist in our culture. Yet both medical and psychological personnel emphasize over and over that masturbation, per se, is not harmful. Some persons still take the position that masturbation is not harmful if it is not excessive. But what is considered excessive? Is the adolescent boy or girl who masturbates daily doing it in excess, especially if that person has made a happy emotional and social adjustment? Masturbation in and of itself is not a problem, but if it becomes a replacement for normal adolescent friendships and social activities, it indicates the person has a problem, not with masturbation, but with social relationships. The wisest course for parents who discover their adolescent boy or girl masturbating is to ignore it. However, if the adolescent seems to be having emotional problems, problems at school, or difficulty in forming friendships, and spends a lot of time alone masturbating, the wise course is to deal with the larger problems of total adjustment rather than with the symptom of masturbation.

Sex therapists now emphasize that one of the greatest helps to sexual responsiveness in marriage is to learn how to masturbate to orgasm. The person who has explored himself or herself, who learns what feels good and what doesn't, who has learned how to become sexually aroused and who knows firsthand the meaning of orgasm, because it has been experienced, is better able to tell his or her married partner how to offer the most effective stimulation. Also, persons who are already orgastic before marriage have far less difficulty in achieving orgasm through intercourse in marriage. McCary in his book *Human Sexuality* writes: "Probably the most successful way of learning to respond to one's full sexual capacity is through self-stimulation." (McCary, 1973, p. 156)

For this reason, many therapists find that for the woman who has never had an orgasm, and who feels too inhibited initially to let her husband pleasure her to bring her to climax, the first task is to instruct her to masturbate when she is alone, and free from fear of interruption or discovery. After orgasm is achieved in this way, and the woman has overcome some of her inhibitions and fears, the next step is for her to learn to become orgastic while stimulated manually by her husband. Finally, in the treatment process, orgasm is attained through intercourse. (See Chapter 16.)

This is not to suggest that masturbation should replace intercourse entirely, Rather, it is to suggest that it is one important way of learning to become sexually responsive. It is to suggest, also, that mutual masturbation should be an important part of love play prior to or even during intercourse.

The anxiety that some persons feel about touching themselves others experience at the thought of their mate touching them. In her book *The New Sex Therapy*, Helen Kaplan describes the case of a couple who had been married eight years without the marriage being sexually consummated. The couple got along well in all other respects. They were gentle, kind, and considerate of each other, but when the husband tried to touch his wife she became tense, anxious, and sometimes hysterical. She was willing to touch her husband's penis—in fact, she enjoyed this and occasionally masturbated him to orgasm in the early years of marriage. Kaplan goes on to describe the case.

One year after their marriage, they attempted coitus on the insistence of his father. The experience was a disaster for both. Thereafter, he became extremely anxious and tense when she wanted to touch his penis. Not surprisingly the couple avoided sex.

Sensate focus and gentle touching without genital touching were suggested. Because of the anxiety this elicited, it took *eight months* and vigorous therapeutic efforts before they could do this with relative ease. Initially, he was too tense to remove his pajamas during the "pleasuring" sessions. The wife, equally uncomfortable, would take a drink and a long hot bath, grit her teeth and force herself to "endure" the touching. However, they eventually learned to relax and once the anxiety about physical intimacy was dispelled, actual sexual contact took place rather easily a short time later. (Kaplan, 1974, p. 150)

Such a case history illustrates the difficulty of overcoming quite deep-seated fears of being touched and the harm created when such fears are instilled. It has been found that children who are hugged, kissed, and cuddled by their parents become more sexually responsive partners in marriage because they have learned to express love physically. However, this does *not* mean that parents should ever deliberately fondle their children's genitals for purposes of sexual stimulation. It means they should teach them simple and acceptable physical expressions of love. One girl relates:

My parents were very warm, demonstrative people. They hugged and kissed us. My father used to hold me on his lap, cuddle, and rock me by the hour. I loved it. When I got married my husband enjoyed physical contact with me just as much as I did. I think this is why we are so compatible.

FEAR AND ANXIETY

Fear and anxiety are also sexually inhibiting. Fears take many forms. Among them are fear of pregnancy, fear of being hurt, fear of rejection, or fear of being criticized, ridiculed, or laughed at.

Fear of Pregnancy. Fear of pregnancy can be so intense as to keep couples from being able to enjoy sex with each other. In fact, in the days before adequate methods of contraception, couples frequently solved the problem of how not to have any more children by sleeping in separate bedrooms and completely abstaining from sex with each other.

Complete protection from unwanted pregnancy, therefore, is a valuable aid to enjoyable sexual expression. The most reliable method is the pill, but not all women can or should take it. There are some risks, especially in older women. Probably the next most reliable method of birth control is the I.U.D., but not all women can use it. Between 20 and 40 percent of the women who try it either expel it or have it removed because of unpleasant side effects. But for women who can wear it, the rate of failure is only 2 to 3 percent. The condom has always been, and still is, one of the most efficient means of birth control, and has the added advantage of protecting against venereal disease, but some men object, claiming that it interferes with their pleasurable feelings during intercourse. It has a slightly higher failure rate than for women who wear I.U.D.s, but usually because of carelessness (it slips off, or it is reused, so that sperm still enter the vagina). When good quality condoms are purchased, they rarely ever have defects. It has been estimated that one may break once in 150 to 300 occasions. This is usually because deteriorated "rubbers" or those of cheap quality are used.

The diaphragm and spermicidal jelly, properly fitted, is regaining popularity as an effective method of birth control.

Many women's groups are urging a return to the diaphragm. As already mentioned, however, the ballooning out of the interior vaginal walls under sexual excitation may cause the diaphragm to loosen, allowing the sperm to leak through around the edges. It is important, therefore, that a physician prescribe as tight a fit for the woman as she can wear and keep in place. When properly fitted, and used with spermicidal jelly, cream, or foam, the failure rate is from 4 to 10 percent.

Vasectomy for couples who already have the normal complement of children, and for husbands who can accept it, should be seriously considered. (See Chapter 4 for additional discussion.) Properly done, it provides 100 percent protection, as does female sterilization. The latter, however, is a much more expensive and more complicated procedure, although the newer methods of sterilization by laparoscopy are less complicated and do not require major surgery. Other attempts at birth control, such as contraceptive foams, creams, or jellies used alone, the rhythm method, withdrawal, or douching, are not reliable. Estimates of the failure rate of the chemicals run from 32 to 50 percent, with the lower rates achieved with the foam. On the average, rhythm may reduce pregnancies by 50 percent, with some women able to use it much more efficiently. Withdrawal has a failure rate of 18 to 23 percent, depending upon the care and timing of the man. Douching is only slightly better than nothing. In fact, it may push the sperm farther up into the vagina or into the cervix. As a group, therefore, these methods ought not to be considered by the couple who are serious about avoiding pregnancy.

Where does this leave us? Each method has certain advantages, disadvantages, and risks. Recently, an analysis was made of various birth control methods from the point of view of health risks—including the risk to health from pregnancy itself. The graph (p. 90) shows deaths per 100, 000 women, for each birth control method, charted in relation to the age of the woman. As can be seen, only the

DEATHS CAUSED BY VARIOUS CONTRACEPTIVE METHODS
Including Deaths from Pregnancies That Result from Contraceptive Failure

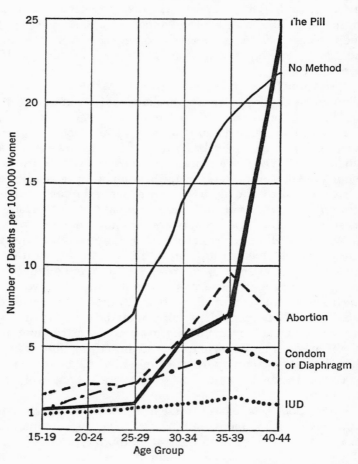

Source: The Population Council

Adapted from "Birth Control Deaths," *Newsweek,* March 1, 1976, p. 60.

pill, condom, diaphragm, I.U.D., and abortion are included in the graph. For women who can wear one, the lowest risk at all ages is the I.U.D. The next lowest risk up to age twenty-nine is the pill; the next lowest risks up to age twenty-nine are the condom and the diaphragm. Note that risk of death from pregnancy is greater than the risk of death from any and all methods of birth control, including abortions, at all age levels, except for the risk of death from the pill after age thirty-nine. The condom and the diaphragm are wise choices for women age thirty and beyond, even though they are not as efficient as the pill. ("Birth Control Deaths," *Newsweek*, March 1, 1976) Abortion is usually not considered a primary means of birth control, for moral and ethical reasons, although it may have to be considered by some as a backup measure in case of the failure of other methods of birth control. The graph leaves out male and female sterilization, but these ought to be given very careful consideration by couples. The chemical means, because of their high failure rate, probably ought to be used only in conjunction with other methods, such as the diaphragm or the condom. All that any couple can do to minimize the fear of pregnancy is to use the most efficient method available consistent with their situation, realizing that not all persons can use all methods.

Fear of Being Hurt. This deterrent to sexual response is especially prevalent early in marriage.

Joan K. was only seventeen years old when she married. One year later her marriage had still not been consummated. When she saw her husband's erect penis she was badly frightened every time he came near her. She had heard stories from girl friends about how it hurt to have intercourse. She was certain she was too small and afraid her husband would hurt her. Finally, her parents took her to a physician, who ruptured her hymen and who reassured her of her capacity to receive her husband's organ

quite easily. Intercourse was finally accomplished, and
Joan began to enjoy it immensely. Years later she wondered why she had ever been so frightened.

It is true that the hymen of some women is quite thick and
inelastic, difficult and painful to rupture. One wife recalled:

> When I first had intercourse, I bled an awful lot. Blood
> was all over the bed. Sex was painful for me for at least the
> first year. After that I had my first orgasm and began to
> enjoy it.

This particular wife was told by her physician that her sexual
organs were quite undeveloped for her age (twenty years). In
fact, her organs were more like those of a young girl. This is
why it took so long to overcome painful intercourse.

Most women experience some or slight pain at the first
intercourse; others have no difficulty at all. There are several
things a couple can do to minimize discomfort. One is for the
couple to make certain the wife is fully aroused, almost to the
point of orgasm, before intromission takes place. Full arousal
will assure natural lubrication within the vaginal orifice.
Two, in addition, the male can use a vaginal jelly on his penis
before inserting it. And three, the male needs to enter cau-
tiously and gently, pushing easily back and forth until intromission is achieved. The wife may be sore for several days
after the hymen is ruptured, and not feel like intercourse,
but the couple can still feel free to stimulate each other by
hand. As soon as the torn hymen is healed, intromission may
be resumed. Initial pain at intercourse gradually subsides as
the vaginal walls stretch. If pain persists, they should see
their physician. Dyspareunia (painful intercourse) is discussed more in detail in a separate chapter.

Sometimes a fear of being hurt develops out of traumatic
experiences which happen while growing up. The young girl
who has been raped or molested, if truly hurt or badly frightened, takes this fear into her marriage. Recently, a young
wife in her late twenties recalled some of the experiences of
her childhood.

My own father first molested me when I was five years old. From that time on until I was fourteen he had intercourse with me regularly. You can imagine what it first felt like when I was young. My vagina was completely undeveloped. I felt as though I was being torn apart.

My first marriage ended in divorce. I couldn't let my husband go near me. All I could think of was those times my father raped me, and how much it hurt.

I'm happily married now, though, and was able to overcome my problem. Before we ever had intercourse, my husband just lay beside me, holding me close to him all night. He did this for several nights, until I began to feel warm, loved, and less frightened. Gradually we began love play, and finally one night I asked him to make love to me. He was wonderful. After that I was never afraid again.

Fear of Rejection. Fear of being repulsed, rejected, turned away, becomes a strong deterrent to the emotionally sensitive person. Sometimes this fear develops only after repeated episodes of actual rejection. One wife related:

Early in our marriage I often took the initiative and indicated to Bob I felt like making love. Sometimes he accused me of being a "sex pot," a "nympho," or "oversexed." At other times he didn't say anything. He just ignored me and turned over and went to sleep. I swear I will never become the aggressor again. If he wants me, he's going to have to come looking for me.

The sad thing about the above case was that the husband never did become the aggressor. The wife remained frustrated for years of married life.

At other times the fear of rejection develops before marriage in the parent-child relationship. A girl who was never secure in her father's love, whose father was detached and insensitive, who couldn't count on his help, acceptance, or approval, may enter marriage with similar attitudes toward her husband. Before a women can give herself completely to her husband, she must have a feeling of trust that he will meet her dependency needs and need for security, that she can depend upon him, that he will take care of her, will be loyal to her and not abandon her. But if her needs were not met by her own father while she was growing up, she may have a deep-seated distrust of her husband from the beginning of marriage. She may have sexual difficulty either because she withholds herself because she does not trust him and does not want to become vulnerable or dependent on him, or because she may be so concerned with pleasing him and serving him (to win his approval) that she allows herself no pleasure in the sexual union. In such a situation, the husband needs to be supersensitive to his wife's anxieties and extremely careful to avoid any actions or conversation that imply disapproval and rejection.

Fear of Performance. One of the most powerful deterrents to effective sexual functioning, especially in males, is fear of failure to perform. A husband who grows the least bit anxious about his potency, who is laughed at, shamed, or otherwise met with a hostile reaction on the part of his wife, may indeed fail. From this point on, his fear of failure evokes almost paranoid reactions, so he does everything possible to avoid sexual humiliation. If, however, an occasional failure is met with love, reassurance, or nonchalance on the part of his wife, so the husband does not have to feel inadequate or afraid, the possibility of sexual failure from that time on is greatly diminished.

Couples need to recognize that no one can supply "instant sex" all the time. Unreasonable or inconsiderate demands, and then ridicule or scorn when they are not met, are often the beginnings of sexual avoidance and sexual failure. When a wife or a husband is nonorgasmic on occasion, they need to recognize that this is quite usual for most couples, and so gloss over it because it is of little significance.

What couples need most to be sexually responsive is approval and acceptance: unqualified love, acceptance, reassurance, and approval.

7

DISTURBED MARRIAGE AND SEXUAL PROBLEMS

THE INFLUENCE OF MARRIAGE ON ONE'S SEXUAL LIFE

The Importance of Feelings. The quality of one's marriage relationship influences one's sexual life. But the quality of the marital relationship depends more on how couples feel toward each other than on any other factors. Are they deeply in love? Are their emotions positive feelings of warmth and affection? Do they truly admire, respect, and accept each other? Do they really show care and concern for each other? If these feelings exist in their relationship, it is not difficult for them to express their love, affection, and admiration through sexual intercourse. If they truly care and show concern for each other, it is also quite a natural thing to accept the other's sexual overtures and to want to respond in a way that will most please.

There have been a number of research studies to determine the causes of marital unhappiness. One study of 984 men and women in intact Catholic marriages revealed 333 problems that could be associated with marital unhappiness. A large portion of these problems could be grouped under five categories. (Mathews and Mihanovich, 1963)

Excessive criticism—My mate tries to hurt my feelings; my mate makes me feel worthless, criticizes me too much, finds fault, nags me, rarely compliments me, and magnifies my faults so that I feel I am unappreciated; I can't please my mate.

Unloved—I desire more affection; I feel unloved and neglected; my mate does not show love; there has been a decline in affection for my mate.

Uncommunicative—I can't talk to my mate; I keep things to myself; we don't discuss anything or confide in each other; we often refuse to speak to each other for hours; my mate won't listen to my opinions; my mate is not open to suggestion; my mate believes what he (she) wants to believe; my mate does not share experiences, I need someone to confide in.

Selfish, inconsiderate—I have to give in more than my mate; I have to cater to my mate's wishes; my mate is inconsiderate and insensitive to my needs and thinks only of his (her) own pleasure.

Other personality traits—My mate can't accept criticism, is stubborn, moody, has frequent temper outbursts, is not grown up, is emotionally immature, likes to argue, is too bossy or acts superior, sulks or holds grudges, or is unhappy much of the time.

An examination of the problems of these couples reveals that negative interpersonal relationships or basic personality faults were the most common types of problems. There was too much criticism, not enough love and expression of affection, a basic lack of communication, or a partner who was selfish, inconsiderate, immature, or otherwise difficult to get along with. When couples have these kinds of negative feelings toward each other, it is difficult to express positive feelings of affection through sex. Such feelings just don't exist. When couples begin to have serious problems, and they are at all sensitive, one of the things they begin to do is withhold affectionate relations. They are angry with each other, so they don't feel like embracing or kissing. They may begin to sleep in separate beds or bedrooms. Of course, withholding sex just adds fuel to the fires of discontent. They begin to feel even more estranged, hostile, or bitter, and that creates more arguments, and conflict, which, in turn, makes them feel even less like sex than before.

Sexual Sabotage. When marital relationships become disturbed, and marital interactions are motivated by hostility, couples often engage in subtle sexual sabotage. The goal is to frustrate the other person's desire for sex. One way is by creating tension: picking quarrels, making demands, criticizing and insulting the other, or by bringing up anxiety-provoking topics such as financial troubles so that the other person gets upset and doesn't feel like intercourse. One wife commented: "If I'm tired and don't feel like sex, I start an argument, my husband gets mad, storms out of the house to the corner bar, and lets me alone." A husband remarked: "All I have to do to turn my wife off is to tell her she's getting fat, or tell her she's a lousy mother, and she forgets all about making love." Other effective devices for pressuring one's partner so he or she can't function are: tell your partner to hurry up, let your partner know that he (or she) is not pleasing but don't tell what will please, let your partner know that you're afraid he won't be potent or that she won't have an orgasm.

Ordinarily, couples who desire a romantic relationship make themselves as appealing as possible: they bathe regularly, make careful use of deodorants or cosmetics, exercise regularly and watch their diet, dress appealingly, are careful about their grooming. Their whole attitude is: I want to be as attractive as possible so you will love me. But couples who do not desire romantic encounters do the opposite: they either consciously or unconsciously destroy their own sexual appeal so their mate will not want sex with them. Such persons become fat, dirty, sloppy in dress and appearance, and completely neglect their grooming and toilet. It is no surprise if a wife is turned off when she gets in bed with a husband who is fat, oily, smelly, and unbathed, who has not brushed his teeth, and who smells up his breath with a before-bed cocktail or with one last cigar.

Couples also become adept at making excuses. The husband can always say he is too busy, that he has some work at the office which he has to finish up. The wife develops a headache; she's too tired; she thinks she hears the baby cry; it's too soon after her period. One wife would keep her husband waiting until 2 A.M. "to be certain the children were asleep." By that time he was so tired he didn't feel like sex then, or he had already fallen asleep.

Even if persons reluctantly agree to intercourse, they can effectively sabotage the sexual relationship by making sex so unpleasant that the wishes of their mates are frustrated. Here are some tactics couples use:

He likes her to swing her hips; she lies motionless.

She likes her breasts caressed; he won't bother, or tells her they are not attractive.

He likes to feel she really needs him; she performs sex disinterestedly, perfunctorily, "to do him a favor."

She likes a period of love play first; he insists on copulation immediately and on "getting it over with."

He likes to see her naked body; she dresses in the fullest, most difficult nightgown to remove.

She wants and needs clitoral stimulation; he implies that other women don't have to have that to have an orgasm.

He likes to experiment; she implies that he is perverted.

She hates television; he must finish the late, late show before making love.

Over a period of time, such tactics will destroy all motivation, which is of course what the other partner wants. Unfortunately, however, such tactics also destroy all feelings of warmth and affection.

Sex as a Weapon. Sex is not always used as an expression of love. It is sometimes used as a weapon to control the other's behavior, to force compliance, or even to hurt and to punish.

Mr. and Mrs. M. came to their minister because of problems in their marriage. The husband had inherited a large farm from his father, which was left to him in his name.

The wife had asked her husband to put it in both their names—in joint ownership—so that if anything happened to the husband, she wouldn't have so many legal problems selling it and wouldn't have to pay an inheritance tax on it. He refused. "No, I won't," was his reply. "It's my farm; it's been in our family for generations. You have no right to it."

Because of her husband's attitude, the wife decided that two could play that game. "All right," she said, "if you won't give me half title to the farm, I won't sleep with you. You can go sleep in your own bed."

This situation had been going on for several months prior to their seeking help from their minister. The clergyman tried to get the couple to work out a solution, but neither would give in. "If you continue in this way, you're going to wreck your marriage completely," was his warning. But to no avail. As far as is known, neither person ever gave in.

Withholding sex as a means of trying to force compliance, or to control the other person's behavior, is highly destructive to the relationship. Even if one person succeeds in getting the other to agree, such tactics create a great deal of resentment and hostility. Consciously or unconsciously, many couples use sex in this way. One wife would not sleep with her husband unless he agreed to buy her a new dress. Another withdrew sex to force her husband to raise her allowance. One husband agreed to make love to his wife if she agreed to clean out the garage for him. In these examples, sex becomes a club to hold over the other person's head, or it becomes payment for acquiescence or for services rendered. One wife was able quite effectively to force her husband to do household chores by threatening to withhold sex if he did not. Saturday night was sex night—if the husband hadn't finished the chores, his wife wouldn't sleep with him until he did.

Sex is also sometimes used to punish, as a means of hurting, as an expression of hostility. How many husbands —in a moment of rage—have forced themselves on their wives without contraceptive protection and have impregnated them deliberately as punishment for real or fancied wrongdoing? Other husbands keep their wives pregnant to "keep them home." It is well known that rape is not an act of lust, but of hate, a way of exerting one's power over another person, to show "superiority," to express deep hostility. Unfortunately, there are husbands who rape their wives in the same way. For the most part, the law says that it is the husband's perogative and that providing sex is the wife's conjugal duty.

The more serious of the previous examples represent an almost complete breakdown of affectionate relationships between husbands and wives. Before a marriage deteriorates to this point, it is hoped that the couple will seek professional assistance.

THE INFLUENCE OF SEX ON MARRIAGE

Sex as Cause. Not all sexual difficulties are due to disturbed marital relationships. Sometimes the opposite is true: the marriage becomes disturbed only after sexual problems develop. Couples carry into their marriage previously acquired sexual attitudes and habits. They have sexual problems from the beginning, not because of a bad marriage but because of individual hang-ups within themselves. The trouble is, unless these are overcome, an otherwise good marriage becomes a disturbed marriage. Sex is too powerful a drive to remain frustrated. If problems persist over a period of time, it affects marital harmony.

One young couple are having sexual problems in their marriage primarily because the wife is inorgastic. She has never experienced orgasm in her five years of marriage, nor ever did prior to marriage. She is willing to sleep with her husband. In fact, she is warm and affectionate with him, and so he feels no real pressure to encourage her to seek help. She has never known the pleasures of orgasm, and therefore, while she knows intellectually that something is wrong, emotionally she doesn't know what she is missing, and thus feels no real pressure either to get help. They have read several good books, but have not gone beyond that to seek assistance.

What is the prognosis of the marriage? It is impossible to predict. But one of several outcomes is likely. The couple may continue the present situation their entire married life and continue to be happily married, as they are now. The wife may eventually resent the fact that her husband wants her to have intercourse when she doesn't get anything out of it. She may end up feeling used and resentful. Or the husband may feel cheated out of the pleasure of seeing his wife respond, may begin to feel that she doesn't care enough to get help, and may resent the fact that she's nonorgasmic and won't do anything about it. He may even feel resentful that she seems to be holding back, even though at this stage her condition is certainly not deliberate or desired. The husband is a very "straight," moral person. It is doubtful that he would ever seek sex outside of marriage; he is more likely to bury himself in his work, and the couple may drift apart. So even if the marriage is still intact, the couple may not maintain the close, warm, affectionate relationship they enjoyed at the beginning of their marriage.

Multiple, Interrelated Problems. An analysis of 1,412 help-request letters sent to the American Association of Marriage Counselors revealed the close relationship between sexual adjustment and other aspects of marriage. This survey revealed three major categories of problems that occurred most frequently. (DeBurger, 1967)

Affectional relations—Spouse is cold, unaffectionate, not in love with me, attracted to and flirts with others, in love with another; I have no feelings for spouse; my spouse is insanely jealous.

Sexual relations—Sexual relations are unsatisfactory; we have insufficient coitus; we have problems with orgasm inability, fridity, or impotence; my spouse wants "unnatural" sex relations.

Personality relations—My spouse is domineering, selfish, irresponsible and undependable, withdrawn, moody, neurotic, has violent temper tantrums, is quarrelsome, bickering, nagging; we are incompatible and have a clash of personalities; I am unstable or have a poor personality.

Fewer couples mentioned such problems as in-laws, religion, drinking, loose sex, gambling, finances, physical illness, failure to meet physical needs, role disagreement, or parental discipline and parent-child conflict. In most cases, couples were experiencing multiple problems: if they had sexual problems, they also felt estranged from each other, or criticized each other for basic faults or for little things. The longer the marriages continued, the greater the problems became.

Other research emphasizes that groups of problems occur together. A husband's lack of sexual interest in his wife may be correlated with quarreling, lack of communication, infidelity, mental health problems, alienation, or other things. A wife's lack of sexual interest in her husband may be correlated with a dislike for her husband, indifference about the marriage, lack of communication, mental health problems, or difficulties in money management, or other problems.

Which comes first: sex problems or unhappy marriage? Either may be the initial contributing cause of the other, but usually they are mutually contributive.

REPAIRING THE RELATIONSHIP

If marital harmony is to be restored, several things have to be done.

Catharsis. Negative feelings toward each other must be "drained off" so they can be replaced by positive feelings. Restoring positive feelings requires first a period of catharsis, where the hurt, anger, hostility, anxiety, or fear is ventilated. Whenever intense negative feelings exist, they alone will prevent the development of positive relationships.

However, it is destructive to the marital relationship for spouses to vent their feelings to each other so they hurt each other's feelings in the process. It is one thing for a husband to say to a counselor: "I can't stand the way my wife dresses," but it's quite another thing for him to tell *her* that. In many cases, therefore, couples ought to vent their negative feelings only to counselors, who can be objective and who don't have to be on the defensive or to take sides. If couples can quarrel *constructively*—which is attacking problems and issues rather than each other—they may be able to work things out themselves, but if their quarreling is *destructive*—which is attacking each other, undermining the ego of each other— they will only add to their difficulties. In this case, they ought to get help.

The following is an example of a constructive quarrel, taken from the author's book on marriage.

> HE *(testy):* "The bank called and said we've overdrawn again."
>
> SHE *(skeptical):* "Gee, darling, I can't believe it. I thought we had plenty of money in our account. Have they made an error?"
>
> HE: "I don't know, but let me see the bankbook."
>
> SHE *(after retrieving the checkbook from her purse):* "We had plenty of money in last week."
>
> HE *(examining the book):* "Didn't you write a check for the insurance? I don't see it."
>
> SHE *(shocked):* "Oh my gosh. I forgot to deduct the $340. No wonder we're overdrawn. I wrote another check to the oil company on top of that."
>
> HE *(sighing):* "What am I going to do with you?"
>
> SHE *(putting her arms around him and kissing him):* "Love me."
>
> HE *(squeezing her hand):* "I do. I do."

The above situation could have resulted in a heated argument if not handled correctly. Note that the couple stick to the issue, without belittling anyone or attacking each other's ego. They discussed in a rational manner, so the wife could admit her mistake without threat. The husband accepted her explanation, with the result that there was a feeling of closeness and love.

Destructive arguments attack the ego rather than the problem, often straying far from the issue at hand. As a result, they create more bitterness, don't solve anything, and leave the couple even more estranged. The following illustrates destructive quarreling. (From the author's book on marriage, with some adaptations.)

THE SCENE: Around the kitchen table in the Smith domicile on Saturday morning following a Friday night dance.

THE CHARACTERS: Sue and Bill Smith

SUE *(sarcastically):* "You were quite a ladies' man at the party last night."

BILL *(casually):* "What do you mean?"

SUE *(raising her voice):* "Get off it. You know good and well what I mean. You danced with Joan half the night. I thought you'd squeeze her so hard you'd smash her boobs."

BILL *(cuttingly):* "Well, at least she's got some to squeeze; that's more than some people I know."

SUE *(starting to yell):* "Look who's talking, lover boy. You couldn't make it last night, could you. What's the matter, loosing your zip?"

BILL *(angrily):* "Not really. You're getting so fat, you're disgusting to look at. Why don't you go see your doctor and lose some weight?"

SUE *(very sarcastically):* "Speaking of doctors, your mother says it's time for your annual checkup. Can't you even go to your doctor without mama reminding you? I never heard of a grown man who calls his mama everyday the way you do."

BILL *(stomping out of the room):* "What does my mother have to do with it? I'm going to play golf."

SUE *(yelling after him):* "Maybe you can score at the country club. You sure can't in bed."

Certainly this quarrel was destructive and did not solve any problems. Sue was jealous and hurt by her husband dancing with Joan, but instead of relieving her anxiety, he tried to belittle her for being flat-chested. She struck back, bringing up his impotence the night before. They each then brought up other subjects: her overweight, his mother, each lashing out at the other. Finally, he retreated to the golf course, and she shouted additional insults at him as he left. Such a quarrel only left them more bitter, increased their misunderstanding and alienation. If couples are not able to quarrel constructively, they need outside counseling help.

Of course, catharsis can be accomplished by other means: work, physical exercise and recreation, social activities, sleep, or constructive outlets such as hobbies or volunteer service. All mature people need to find socially acceptable means of expressing tension. Sometimes, after intense negative feelings have subsided, the couple can return to the problem and solve it easily. Sometimes, a good night's sleep will do more to relieve tension than an all-night battle.

Of course, sex itself can be cathartic. If couples have deserted their marriage bed, if they can bring themselves to start having intercourse again, this in and of itself is a healing process and develops more affectionate feelings. So it is helpful if they resume sexual relations just as soon as their feelings do not completely bar such resumption.

Sex therapists have sometimes been accused of focusing on the sexual relationship to the exclusion of other marital problems. In her book on *The New Sex Therapy,* Kaplan writes:

Often it is possible to "bypass" marital problems. Nodal points of trouble are identified and the couple is charged

with the responsibility of "keeping them out of their bedroom" prior to final resolution. "You can have your choice
—fight or make love tonight. But don't try to do both. It
probably won't work." (Kaplan, 1974, p. 168)

Kaplan does go on to say, however, that sometimes bypassing
the problem won't work: sexual improvement will not take
place until the interactional problem is improved.

Gaining Insight. Often, disturbed couples are not aware of
the real basis of their difficulty. They pick on little things
without getting at the real roots of their problem. This is not
deliberate. It is just that feelings prevent clear thinking, or
they have built up so many ego defenses that they no longer
are able to sort out truth from error. Most people begin to
show a "halo effect," to declare themselves innocent and
their mate at fault. "If only my wife (or husband) would do
this or that, then everything would be all right." "It's not my
fault," is frequently heard by marriage counselors. One of the
purposes of counseling is to help couples gain insight, and for
each to assume part of the responsibility for their problems.
The more they talk, the more insightful they become and the
more they are willing to admit that they too may be partly
at fault.

If insight is to be obtained, it is necessary for couples to
restore communication, to begin talking to each other in
reasonable ways. Disturbed marriage indicates a breakdown
of communication. Most counselors would agree that if they
can just get couples talking about their problem, the relationship can be improved. The most effective means of solving
problems is honest, but tactful, and rational discussion. Un-
willingness to talk or to listen stands as a barrier to communication.

Motivation, Negotiation, and Compromise. Couples also
have to want to improve their relationships by being willing
to negotiate and to make compromises. The wife who wants

her husband home more, the husband who wants his wife to go out with him more, have to compromise somehow. If the conflict ends up with one or the other always giving in, resentment results. If, of course, first one then the other acquiesces, the results are at least equitable.

Nothing requires more consideration than making satisfactory sexual adjustments. Each person must be completely considerate of the other's feelings, and in meeting the other's needs, yet without completely squelching all self-desire and self-fulfillment. Above all, solving sexual differences requires a considerable degree of unselfish consideration, and cooperative, mutual efforts to succeed. This is why sex is a good measure of the kind of person you are as well as of the things you do. More will be said about solving sexual differences in the next chapter.

PART II

DIFFERENCES
IN SEXUAL PREFERENCES

8

DIFFERENCES
IN THE DESIRED FREQUENCY
OF SEXUAL RELATIONS

HOW often should couples have sexual intercourse? As often as they want to. But what if they differ on how often that should be? That, then, becomes a problem.

One of the most frequently asked questions relates to the frequency of intercourse. Whenever I'm asked this in a couples group, I feel trapped. A number of persons present hope I'll indicate "very often"; others hope I'll support their feelings by giving some figure that represents infrequent relations. Whatever figures I report, I make someone unhappy.

THE NUMBERS GAME

Averages. Although there is the risk of disappointing some person, it is helpful to give some general ideas. Just as a starter: What do other couples do? What are the averages? Realizing that all persons are individuals and that they should not try to do what anyone else does, let's look at some figures on frequency of intercourse and at the implications of these statistics. One study of married men showed that frequency varied greatly from person to person. (Pearlman, 1972). In general, younger husbands had intercourse more often than older ones, and most men showed some decline in frequency with advancing age. For example, according to Pearlman, 3 out of 4 married men in their twenties had intercourse 2 to 4 times per week. Among those in their thirties, half of all married men had intercourse 2 to 4 times per week. Among married men in their forties, 43 percent still had intercourse that often, while 31 percent did who were in their fifties. There were still 7 percent of married men in their sixties and 4 percent in their seventies who were still having intercourse 2 to 4 times per week.

What were the percentages of married men who had intercourse at least once a week or oftener? Ninety-three percent of those in their twenties, 82 percent of those in their thirties, 70 percent of those in their forties, 49 percent of those in their fifties, 26 percent of those in their sixties, and 11 percent of those in their seventies had intercourse at least once a week or more often.

What about the percentage of those who had intercourse far less often? The following figures show the percentages of married men in each age group who had intercourse only once per month or less. (Pearlman, 1972)

20–29 years— 3%
30–39 years— 5%
40–49 years— 9%
50–59 years—19%
60–69 years—25%
70–79 years—22%

It is quite obvious that the frequency with which married men had sexual relations declined only slowly with age, that those who had intercourse less often than once a week were in the minority up until age fifty. Those who had intercourse less often than 3 times per month were in the minority until age sixty; those who had intercourse less often than 2 times per month were in the minority until age seventy. Apparently, sexual drive wanes very slowly. Only a little over half of all married men seventy to seventy-nine years of age were completely sexually inactive. (Pearlman, 1972)

Frequency and Satisfaction. One cannot assume that all couples who have intercourse with above-average frequency have better sexual lives and that couples who have relations with below-average frequency have worse ones. The number of times per week or month is not in and of itself the only measure of sexual satisfaction. For example, a wife who has sex daily but who is rarely orgasmic may report far less satisfaction with her sexual life than one who has intercourse once per week, but always has an orgasm. Some couples who report below-average frequency also report above-average satisfaction. Overall, however, those who have frequent intercourse are more likely to report satisfaction with their sexual lives than those who have infrequent intercourse. In a *Redbook* magazine survey of the sexual lives of 100,000 married women, 7 out of 10 women who had intercourse 6 to 10 times per month reported their sexual lives as good or very good, but among those who had intercourse 16 or more times per month, 9 out of 10 reported satisfying sexual lives (good or very good). However, there were still 35 percent of those who had intercourse only 1 to 5 times per month who also found their sexual lives satisfying. (Levin and Levin, 1975)

An equally important factor in satisfaction is frequency of orgasm. In the *Redbook* magazine survey, 8 out of 10 women who were orgasmic all or most of the time reported satisfaction with marital sex, but only half of those who were only sometimes orgasmic reported satisfaction. It is significant, though, that over one fourth of those who were never orgasmic also rated their sexual lives as satisfying. Apparently, these nonorgasmic women found pleasure in intercourse other than through orgasm. (Levin and Levin, 1975)

If we combine frequency of intercourse and frequency of orgasm, these two factors taken together become one of the most important criteria of sexual satisfaction, not for everyone, but for the majority. Overall, the frequency with which couples make love *and* experience orgasm is directly related to the probability of their reporting a high degree of satisfaction with marital sex.

Desires. The important consideration, however, is not only how often couples have intercourse but how they feel about the frequency with which they are participating. One report of female college graduates whose median age was 26.2 years and who had been married a median period of 4.2 years revealed that 69 percent felt that their frequency of intercourse was about right, 6 percent said it was too frequent, and 25 percent said it was too infrequent. (Bell, 1972) The percentage of wives who complain that sexual relations are too infrequent has been increasing over the years. In previous generations, this complaint most likely came from the husbands. The wives more often complained of too frequent sexual relations. Now this is no longer true. These changes reflect the differences between women today and those of yesteryear. Modern women feel much freer to express their sexuality, but this is putting a lot more pressure on their husbands, some of whom can't or won't fulfill their needs.

INFREQUENT INTERCOURSE

Discovering Reasons. If an individual desires intercourse so infrequently that there is a marked difference in desire between the husband and the wife, the first task is to get at causes. Why does one person desire intercourse infrequently?

Physical factors should be checked first. Sexual hormone deficiencies, illness, physical fatigue, the use of drugs that might have a sedative or inhibiting effect, are all possible causes. Also, has the person always had an infrequent desire, or is this a radical change in his or her normal pattern? A person who has always wanted frequent sexual relations and then suddenly wants sex less frequently or not at all must have some reason for this. Is this an indication of physical changes that are taking place, or of illness? The answers to these questions need to be determined before the causes can be known.

A second step is to examine *sexual factors* to uncover any elements in the relationship which have resulted in one person's not wanting to have relations at all, or as often. Is sex pleasurable? Are both the husband and the wife orgasmic? Has something happened to "turn off" one of the spouses? Have there been serious disagreements over any aspect of their sexual life in addition to differences in desired frequency? The couple need to examine every aspect of their sexual life together: the manner and mode in which they touch each other, their feelings about their lovemaking techniques and sexual expression, their pleasure or displeasure in seeing each other or not seeing each other, the pleasure or discomfort experienced because of body odors, the influence that physical environment and other environmental circumstances have on their sexual life. Often mates have not been able to tell each other what is bothering them. Rather than do so, one person begins to withdraw from having relations. If the couple can let each other know, sometimes the situation can be remedied. Or, often, a husband or a wife has said something but the other hasn't really understood, or accepted what has been said, so nothing has changed. The important question is: Why is the one person not interested in having sexual relations very often? And can the spouse accept this seriously as a valid reason?

The next step is to examine *psychological factors,* such as the onset of emotional illness or depression, the development of fears, anxieties, or guilt. One husband complained:

> My wife and I have always enjoyed sex together, but lately she has not seemed too interested. When I suggest intercourse, she says she is too tired, or she doesn't feel like it; sometimes she doesn't even appear to hear what I've said. If she is willing, she doesn't have an orgasm like she used to, or she just lies there, letting me do everything, but without really becoming a part of it herself. It's as though her mind is a million miles away. She has seemed very depressed lately. She sits daydreaming by the hour, doesn't do her housework, and lets the kids run wild, or else she gets very upset and cries easily. I don't know what's the matter with her.

The wife in this example was going through a period of mental depression that was affecting not only her sexual life with her husband but most of her daily activities. She needed a doctor's care, and perhaps psychological help.

When people become emotionally depressed, communication with them becomes more difficult; they usually have less interest in sex, or show less frequent orgasmic response.

A fourth step is to examine *marital factors* to determine if disturbance and unhappiness in the marriage is the reason why one person is not interested in sleeping with the other. When asked why she didn't want to sleep with her husband, one wife replied:

> Because I don't like my husband very much. He does so many things I dislike. I'm getting so I can't stand him, and he's not too fond of me either. We seem to have given up trying to please each other. He's still interested in sex, but I don't think he's really interested in me, so I really have no desire to have intercourse with him. This leads to all sorts of arguments, but it is the way I feel.

In the above case, it was difficult to sort out cause and effect. One of the reasons the husband was doing so many things he knew his wife disliked was that she wouldn't sleep with him very often. He did things that annoyed her to get back at her, which made her even more resentful. In this case, marriage counseling and sexual therapy were both needed if the relationship was to improve.

A fifth step is to examine *environmental* or *situational factors* as causes. Is there something in their present circumstances of living which is causing dissatisfaction with the frequency of sexual intercourse? One wife confessed:

> The cause of my frustration is very simple—my husband is never home. He is on the road all of the time with his job, so I don't get to see him very much. Sometimes he gets home Saturday night and sometimes not for two weeks. I never know. I would like him to make love to me several times a week, but how can he? I've asked him to try to get

another job, but he says that's all he knows how to do, and that, besides, he might not get as good pay doing something else. I guess I'll just have to be frustrated, but I don't like it.

Work schedules, or the pressures of work, are a common cause of sexual frustration. One wife complains constantly that her husband, who is a carpenter, comes home so tired at night that he never wants to make love. The husband is very tense, a high-pressure type of man, who has a compulsion about work. He never takes it easy. He works six days a week, and at full speed all day. He says it's the only way he can make any real money. Another wife, whose husband is a business executive, is unhappy because of the demands of her husband's job which requires a lot of night work and many weekends.

Husbands as well as wives are sometimes frustrated. In explaining why he wanted to leave his wife, one husband remarked:

My wife never has any time for me. She works full time, and she joins so many clubs she's never home. She's an officer in a half dozen organizations, is on a lot of committees, and attends a lot of meetings—especially in the evening. I'm lucky to get to see her, much less have a chance to have intercourse. Last month we had intercourse only once the whole month. As far as I'm concerned, I might as well be living somewhere else. If she doesn't want to be a wife to me, I might as well leave.

In such situations, couples have to examine their lives and really begin to think about the order of their priorities. What do they really want out of life? Is work more important than their marriage? Do they really care enough to try to change things? Sometimes it is helpful if busy people actually schedule time together. It may be the only way they will find time to be together. I recently suggested that to a busy businessman. His wife asked: "You mean schedule sex? Isn't that rather unromantic?" Not necessarily. When two people are courting, don't they arrange a time for a date? Does this make it any less exciting because they agree on an appointed time to meet? As a matter of fact, two married people may find that their arranged dates and times together are the most exciting times of the week. They can look forward to those times with eager anticipation. And these dates don't have to be at night. For people who can take an hour off from work, how about an 11 A.M. date at home in the bedroom, followed by lunch? Or, how about intercourse after the kids are off for school, and before going to work? It can be a wonderful beginning to a fine day.

Couples who never have time for each other are putting everything else before their marriage. If that's the way they want it, fine, but if they don't like it and can change their priorities or their schedules and don't, they have only themselves to blame. Often, of course, one person is willing and the other isn't, which is sometimes the problem in the first place. But if people really care, they show their love by trying to fulfill each other's needs. If they don't, they really aren't in love. They have to care enough to do their very best.

Individual Differences. One must recognize that there are individual differences between people and these can create problems, not because there is something wrong with either one of them, but because that is the way the people are. Whether heredity or environment has played the major role in determining their sexual capacities and needs, the fact remains that they aren't necessarily sick, on drugs, emotionally ill, afraid, worried, or guilty. They may be completely orgastic and enjoy sex together; their marriage may otherwise be quite harmonious and their situation such that they do have the time to make love. They simply have differences in their sexual appetites. In this case, they can agree to make compromises without having to solve any major problems ahead of time. As a general rule, one person should not frustrate the desires of the other, unless there are very important reasons for doing so, and even then the occasions of denial should be kept to an absolute minimum.

VERY FREQUENT INTERCOURSE

The Sexual Athlete. There are a few people who have very great sexual appetites, either for a short or for a long period of time. A male friend confided:

> When we were first married, my wife wanted intercourse morning, noon, and night. I think we must have done it 4 or 5 times a day. After the first several days, I was in agony. I was so sore I couldn't walk. Even now, she would prefer making love at least twice a day 7 days a week. She knows I can't that often, but I know she would like to.

It is not unusual for couples to go through a period of weeks or months, especially at the beginning of marriage, when they are sexually very active. They can't seem to get enough of each other. Or they each believe (sometimes falsely) that they should make love that often, or that the other wants them that frequently, and they are afraid to say "no." They don't want to hurt each other's feelings, so they keep on, not really realizing that their marathon of sexual activity has become an ordeal. The solution to the dilemma, of course, is better communication.

Or, individuals may go through periods when their desire is far greater than normal. One man in his middle thirties remarked:

> I'm going through a period when I need a lot of sex: at least two or three times a day. My wife and I have always had intercourse several times a week. But now I want it much more often. My wife's beginning to object, but so far she's been cooperative.

In this example, the husband was going through a period of deep emotional conflict. He started using drugs, seeing another woman, and, during this period, gave up a number of hobbies and recreational pursuits he normally enjoyed. Sex became a means of trying to ease anxiety, of relieving upset, of overcoming insecurity, of solving his conflict. Once his emotional problems were resolved, his sexual life and his interest in other things returned to normal.

In another case, a wife reacted to the changes at menopause by developing an almost insatiable desire for sex. She had to prove to herself over and over that she was still attractive, loved, and, above all, still young. Her markedly increased sexual desires were a symptom of her anxiety about growing older. The change of life represented, for her, a loss of femininity and youthfulness, so she had to prove to herself over and over that these things weren't really happening. In this case, the husband was able, through word and deed, to show his wife how much he loved her and admired her, and to convince her that she was still a beautiful, desirable woman. Her unreasonable desire for sex gradually subsided as her emotional needs were fulfilled. It is not at all unusual for persons to try to fulfill their deep longing for love and approval through sexual means. This is a very important cause of excessive interest in sexual expression.

Sometimes, in males, heightened sexual activity occurs as anxiety about potency increases. The more anxious a man becomes about his manhood, the more he tries to reassure himself that it is not so, by wanting intercourse time and time again. Men too may fear growing older, and seek to reassure themselves through sexual means.

When sex becomes an all-consuming desire and activity, it is also sometimes an attempt to escape. People can try to escape from their problems and worries through sex as well as through sleep, alcohol, or drugs. Many men, especially, use sex as a means of relieving tension. Ordinarily, this is quite a usual response. They're upset or nervous; they want the comfort of their wife's arms, the relief of orgasm. This attempt at sexual relief, however, can sometimes reach exaggerated proportions and become a symptom of very real emotional difficulties. One woman reports that every time she gets nervous, she has the urge to masturbate, which she does, often as much as three or four times a day. She may even go into the woman's toilet at work and masturbate during her coffee break. Sex for her has become a compulsion, a means of trying to relieve unresolved conflicts and problems. Counseling would help her to get at the basis of her problems.

What's Normal? We must be very cautious about suggesting that there is something wrong with the person who wants intercourse every day, or several times a day. There are persons who desire intercourse this frequently for years and years. They seem to be well-adjusted, normal people in every respect. Masters and Johnson tell the story of a couple who came to their St. Louis clinic because the wife could not get pregnant. It was discovered the couple were having intercourse three times every day. When it was explained to them that such a frequency did not allow sufficient time for the husband's sperm count to build up, the couple were persuaded to quit having intercourse for a period of time. They did so. Upon resuming relations, the wife became pregnant, and immediately the couple resumed their "normal" pattern of intercourse three times daily!

Most couples would be exhausted by such sexual activity. But this frequency did not create any problems for the couple because they were both satisfied with it. While the couple could not be considered average, one could not really say they were abnormal.

ACHIEVING HARMONY

Three Approaches. Basically, there are three different approaches to solving the problem of wide differences in the frequency with which couples want to make love. One is to try to increase the frequency of the spouse with the lesser appetite. Many suggestions have already been given. This approach is necessary if basic problems exist which prevent that person from desiring or practicing frequent intercourse. Sexual desire cannot be forced, but it can be released by removing those physical, sexual, psychological, marital, environmental, or situational barriers which prevent full expression. Once the barriers are discovered and broken down, the couple can usually work out an acceptable frequency.

The second approach is to try to decrease the frequency of the partner with the greater appetite. This, however, is risky business. The person with the lesser appetite may already be trying to do this through the various techniques of sexual sabotage described earlier. This only serves to increase tension and resentment. If sexual athleticism is an effort to fulfill emotional or psychological needs, these can be discovered and dealt with by a counselor, or sometimes by the couple themselves. Once the emotional problems are solved, desire declines of its own accord.

The third approach is for the person with the lesser appetite to try to meet the needs of the person with the greater appetite, partly through coitus and partly through noncoital sex. The suggestion has already been made that ordinarily one person should not refuse fairly reasonable requests unless there is some exceptionally good reason for doing so. But it may be that part of the larger appetite will have to be satisfied through masturbation. In his book *Sexual Difficulties in Marriage,* Mace suggests that if one person wants intercourse when the other is not able to respond, the one wanting sex guide the other in masturbating him or her to orgasm. (Mace, 1972) For example, the wife who is desirous of sex may guide her husband's hand as he masturbates her. Or the husband who needs relief will guide his wife's hand as she satisfies him. Mace writes:

> Once a couple can give each other enjoyable and satisfying experiences through noncoital sex, they are no longer dependent on intercourse as the only source of sexual pleasure. At times when intercourse is not possible for any reason, they can still have sexual enjoyment. . . . In her

function as a cook, a wife may on occasion have to express regret that she can't provide her husband with steak, but she can fix him some eggs or some cold chicken— he doesn't have to go hungry. Likewise in her function as a sex partner, she need not feel, when she is unable to match his desire, that the only alternative is sexual starvation. (Mace, 1972, p. 31)

Mace goes on to say that he is not recommending noncoital sex as a way of life for couples, although in certain situations (such as a permanently physically disabled husband) it can be that. But he is suggesting that noncoital sex can take up the slack and overcome the problem of nonmatching sexual patterns.

A female student in the author's marriage class wrote a paper in which she described her decision to marry a man who was completely sexually impotent because of irreparable physical damage. She and her fiancé had discussed the problem quite frankly and had decided that noncoital sex would be their only answer. So while this is not suggested for most people as a substitute for intercourse, it may have to be for some. For others, it may be a supplement to coitus, and quite helpful to the relationship.

9

DIFFERENCES IN THE MODE AND MANNER OF SEXUAL EXPRESSION

BECAUSE of individual differences, it is not uncommon for husband and wife to have disagreements over how they express themselves sexually.

SOME COMMON DISAGREEMENTS

Coital Positions

Mrs. G. is disturbed by her husband's preoccupation with coital positions. He attempts to employ as many as he can think of during a sexual act. The constant shifting distracts the wife and detracts from her pleasure. The husband claims he is "liberated" and that his wife is too old-fashioned.

It is possible to develop an obsession about sexual positions as well as about other things, but an examination of the above case by a counselor revealed the following. The husband liked to begin intercourse in a superior position. If his wife had not climaxed, he preferred rolling over and being on the bottom because he found it less stimulating, and this was one way he could avoid climax and maintain an erection. Sometimes afterward he liked to have intercourse in a side-by-side position facing his wife. Over a period of time, he had suggested to her that they try out a variety of other positions. Partially on and off the side of the bed, in chairs, using pillows, while standing up, bathing, etc. The wife found all of this rather ludicrous and distracting. However, the husband and wife had been married a short time, and the young husband was fascinated and curious about experimentation. At the same time, the wife was rather embarrassed by the different suggestions. Once the initial novelty wore off, and the counselor had encouraged the couple to air their feelings and to discuss the whole situation, the husband's interest in so many different positions tapered off, the wife began to feel somewhat freer and less inhibited, and their sexual relations became more harmonious.

Intercourse During Menstruation. One frequent source of disagreement is over whether or not to have sexual intercourse during menstruation. Actually, the whole idea is shocking to some people. However, there are couples who regularly have relations during menstruation and think nothing of it. Recently a wife complained to her counselor.

> I would like to have intercourse during my period, but my husband won't do it. For one thing, my periods sometimes go on for 7 days or so, and I get very frustrated during this time. For another thing, I feel my husband ought to be able to accept me completely—period and all. I feel he's holding himself back, and not really able to love me as I am.

Upon questioning, the husband replied:

> As far as I'm concerned, intercourse during her period is out. The whole idea really turns me off. It's too messy. I wouldn't think of it.

At this point the counselor explored with the couple the possibility of mutual masturbation. The wife felt this would satisfy her, temporarily; the husband said it was acceptable, particularly since it only involved manipulation of the clitoral area beneath his wife's pad.

Before we discuss the aesthetic and psychological considerations, which many persons feel are the most important factors, what about the medical and health implications? In most cases, intercourse during menstruation is safe, with no adverse physical effects. There are, however, some women who are subject to urinary tract infections or to endometriosis or tubal inflammations. Intercourse during menstruation may increase the possibility. Also, use of acid contraceptive creams, jellies, or foams during menstruation may result in burning sensations and inflammation. This, of course, can be avoided by using other means of contraception. If there are any doubts about the advisability, the couple should consult their physician. Some women find that sexual activity during menstruation relieves cramps, pain, backache, or other discomfort, and thus get considerable relief if they have sex during this time.

Aesthetic or psychological objections are quite pronounced in some couples. Some persons react to the blood flow with considerable anxiety. The increase of vaginal odors during menstruation are enough to turn some husbands off. Many wives aren't in the mood for sex during their periods, while others experience increased drive. A large number of couples find that menstruation neither diminishes nor increases their pleasure and desire, so they proceed with intercourse as usual, perhaps avoiding relations during those days when menstrual flow is exceptionally heavy. Most physicians feel that unless there are specific contraindications because of medical considerations, couples who wish to have relations during menstruation ought to feel free to have them. However, no couples should be pressured into feeling that they ought to. One report by Masters and Johnson of 331 women who took part in an "orgasm during menstruation" study revealed that 33 of the women objected on religious or aesthetic grounds, 173 wanted coitus, especially during the last half of the flow, and the remaining 125 had no special feelings one way or the other. Unfortunately, the study did not include the attitudes of the husbands.

Oral Sex. Whether or not to employ oral-genital stimulation is a decision that each couple have to make for themselves. Studies of modern couples reveal that the overwhelming majority have used this method of stimulation, or would like to try it. The actual percentages of couples who practice it vary from study to study. In Kinsey's research, which was conducted over twenty-five years ago, about half of the women had experienced *fellatio* (the woman stimulating the man's penis), and slightly over half had experienced *cunnilingus* (the man stimulating the female's genitals). (Kinsey, 1953) In the 1975 *Redbook* magazine survey already referred to, 9 out of 10 women had experienced oral-genital sex, both giving and receiving it. Almost half of those participating engaged in it often, and half engaged in it occasionally. Only a few women had had it just once. (Levin and Levin, 1975) These figures are somewhat higher than in a 1973 study of 2,372 married American women which showed that 8 out of 10 wives had oral-genital sex. In general, a greater percentage of younger wives have had oral sex than have older wives, indicating a shift in what is acceptable sexual behavior. (Bell and Connolly, 1973)

Certainly, oral sex should not be called perverted. If it is, then the vast majority of people are perverted. Ordinarily, however, fellatio and cunnilingus are used as part of love play, as a means of sexual excitement prior to intercourse. If they are used all the time as a substitute or replacement for intercourse, usually some problem exists. Some women can have an orgasm only through cunnilingus or through other means of manual stimulation, even though they are willing to participate in intercourse with their husbands. This is not at all an unusual occurrence, and is discussed more in detail in the chapter on orgasm incapacity.

Although oral-genital stimulation is acceptable behavior, the acceptance is predicated on the assumption that both partners want it. Such activities should not be inflicted on one person by the other, but should be mutually desired and enjoyable. If one person tries to push the other into this sexual practice, this represents coercion and an attempt at domination, and is usually deeply resented. However, if encouraging and seductive approaches are made, it may be that the reticent partner will gradually accept the idea. Some such people find they thoroughly enjoy this activity once initial barriers are broken down.

There are several things that increase acceptance. One, be certain the genitals are scrupulously clean. This not only eliminates unpleasant tastes and odors but also the possibility of any contamination of the genitals by fecal matter, which in turn may result in such diseases as infectious hepatitis. Herpes, gonorrhea, and syphilis viruses are not always destroyed by bathing, however, so the possibility of contracting V.D. from an infected person is possible through oral sex as well as through coitus.

Two, for the person who is reticent, oral stimulation is more acceptable after he or she has already become very aroused through other means of stimulation. At the height of sexual passion, oral sex becomes quite pleasurable. At other times, it is unacceptable to some people.

Three, some persons are able to become uninhibited enough to accept oral stimulation only after a cocktail or after smoking marihuana. While some measure of intoxication does minimize inhibitions, these persons usually feel guilty or ashamed after they sober up. If they are going to feel guilty, they ought not to do it.

Certainly, pleasurable or meaningful sexual expression does not depend upon oral-genital contact. If it does, there is something wrong. Most couples can either take it or let it alone. It's not that important—and certainly not vital to a fulfilling sexual life. In other words, even though they use it, they can do without it. The best advice is not to make any big fuss over it. Don't let one's sexual pleasure hinge on whether one does or does not. This is magnifying one type of sexual expression out of all proportion to its significance.

SEXUAL DEVIATIONS

There is a whole category of sexual problems that are best labeled sexual deviations. These are modes and means of sexual expression that are departures from usual forms. Most people would consider such deviations quite "abnormal" or "queer." Some are quite harmful to marital relationships. Others are not too harmful in and of themselves, but create a great deal of dissension or conflict between spouses over their employment.

Anal Intercourse. Anal intercourse, or *sodomy,* is defined here as the insertion of the penis into the rectum. It is strictly forbidden in the Old Testament, where the term is also used to include intercourse with an animal *(bestiality).* Unlike oral-genital stimulation, anal intercourse is not regularly practiced. Large numbers of couples may have tried it, but usually only out of curiosity. Probably fewer than 1 percent have used it often as a regular means of sexual expression. For this reason, it is being included here as a sexual deviation.

Strictly from a physical point of view, there is no question that both men and women can receive sexual stimulation from anal penetration. The female sexual organs and the anus have the same nerve supply, so that the anus can be stimulated sexually in this way. Some male homosexuals practice anal intercourse, but the majority avoid it on a regular basis because of physical pain or because of emotional distaste for the experience. Most married couples have no need of anal intercourse, preferring sex in the usual way.

The unusual person, however, prefers anal intercourse over vaginal coitus. This may be due to early childhood conditioning. Mothers who give frequent and unnecessary enemas to children may, unwittingly, be conditioning them to enjoy this type of sexual satisfaction. Some children experiment with sticking things into their anus. If this practice persists into adulthood, they may desire such activity after marriage.

There are some real dangers to health from the practice of anal intercourse. The most persistent organism invading and infecting a women's vagina originates in the bowel. If the husband penetrates the vagina following anal intercourse, he may infect his wife with his bacterially contaminated penis. The most common injury from anal intercourse is a split or crack in the anal canal, due to the relatively large diameter of the penis. Occasionally, a crack develops into a full anal fissure. Anal intercourse may also damage previously existing conditions such as hemorrhoids. Less commonly, the penis suffers painful abrasion. Ordinarily, there are no compelling reasons why married couples should have to resort to anal intercourse to gain sexual pleasure and satisfaction. In fact, among those who have tried it, it is usually listed as the least liked of various types of sexual activity. If one person persists contrary to the desires and feelings of the other, counseling help should be sought.

Transvestism. This is the practice, in males, of obtaining sexual stimulation and/or satisfaction by wearing clothes of the female sex. One wife described her husband in this way.

> My husband enjoys wearing women's panties and stockings when we have intercourse. He gets very excited when he puts them on, and comes very quickly. I was really shocked when he first did this; I think he's queer.

If one is to judge by the many wives who write in to Ann Landers about their transvestite husbands, the deviation is fairly common. Some of these wives have learned to accept their husbands aberrations; others are completely disgusted by them. One wife said she even went shopping for lace panties and other lingerie for her husband, who regularly wore these under his own clothes. This wife even washed and cared for his things! Her attitude was: "It doesn't really harm anyone, so why should I mind? He enjoys it so, I wouldn't think of asking him to give it up." Most wives are not able to be this accepting of a practice they consider indicative of homosexuality.

Actually, transvestites may be *heterosexuals, bisexuals,* or *homosexuals.* The majority are usually not homosexuals. Married men who seem perfectly normal in every other way who prefer sexual relations with their wives rather than with men are heterosexuals in spite of this deviancy.

The deviance usually can be traced back to childhood. Classically, the parents attempt to overcome their disappointment that their boy is not a girl by dressing him in feminine clothing. The boy grows up feeling he can gain more approval and acceptance by dressing in girl's attire. In marriage, this actually becomes a way of gaining his wife's approval, or of overcoming insecurity and anxiety about his masculinity.

Or, while growing up, a boy may playfully dress up in his mother's or sister's clothes. In so doing, he attracts attention and comments of approval. This happens innocently and is not a cause for alarm. However, if the desire to dress up in girl's clothing persists, particularly if accompanied by a preference of girls for playmates and by a desire to grow up to be a woman, parents ought to consider getting an expert's opinion. The more intense and persistent the desire to dress in girl's clothing, the more attached the boy becomes to this type of behavior, the more concerned parents should be about the prognosis. In extreme forms, boys who prefer to wear feminine clothing all the time, who take the role of the female in playing house or other games, who try to imitate women in the way they walk or talk, clearly exhibit a disorder of gender orientation called *transsexualism.* These are the persons who as adults may seek surgical sex changes, since they actually consider themselves kept prisoner in a body of the wrong sex.

The male transvestite feels that he is a man, although he enjoys fantasying himself as a woman. He gets pleasure out of secretly dressing in feminine attire and in remaining undetected by the outside world. When he reveals his fettish to his wife, he is protecting himself against his masculine inadequacy and his fear of being rejected by a female. With his masculinity disguised by his dress, he feels freer in indulging in and enjoying genital activity. He doesn't "dare" as a man, because of fear of rejection or disapproval.

The transvestite husband is a problem to the wife who is repelled by his behavior. In such cases, the couple would do well to seek psychotherapy. In extreme cases, transvestites dress completely as women and go out in public in feminine attire. If caught, they can be prosecuted, and cause embarrassment to the family. A transvestite differs from the effeminate homosexual who parodies women by wearing feminine attire in a grotesque way. The latter hates women and does not wish to appear like normal women, whom he dislikes. The transvestite likes women and fantasizes himself as one of them.

Voyeurism. The *voyeur* is commonly the "peeping tom" who secretly enjoys looking at others while they are undressing, nude, or engaging in sexual activity. Most commonly the voyeur is a male, since according to FBI reports, 9 men to every 1 woman are arrested on charges of "peeping." The voyeur becomes a problem to himself and to his friends and family because of the illegal nature of his activities.

Actually most persons have some voyeuristic tendencies. Growing children manifest a certain interest in seeing each other naked. Such childhood games as "doctor" have voyeuristic overtones. Most married spouses are curious about seeing each other naked or undressing, and find such demonstrations sexually stimulating. It has already been suggested that most couples find making love "with the light on" sexually stimulating. Some adults even view sexually oriented material before coitus. Others enjoy burlesque shows or sexual activity in movies. Thus, in its broadest sense, voyeurism is any effort to obtain sexual stimulation or satisfaction through any visual perception of sexually stimulating objects or persons. Is the male who likes to look at *Playboy* magazine a voyeur? In this sense, yes.

In this broader sense, then, voyeurism must be considered normal. However, whether it becomes abnormal or not depends upon the particular types of behavior, the appropriateness of that behavior, the acceptance of it by other individuals and by society. The husband who enjoys watching his wife undress is quite normal, but one who enjoys sneaking through backyards to peek in windows to see other women undressing rather than having intercourse with his wife is evidencing deviant behavior, as is the husband in the following case.

> Bonnie P. came to her doctor quite upset because of her husband's strange behavior. Her husband would try to sneak out of the house and go to his wife's bedroom window to observe her undressing without her knowing it. When she caught him she told him he could see her undress by staying indoors, that she didn't mind, but he kept sneaking out to observe her secretly.

As is so often true, the voyeurism in the above example is quite deviant behavior because it has become a replacement for, or substitute for, the real thing. It became quite a problem to the wife, who was very frightened and upset by her husband's activity.

In another case, a wife described how her husband wanted her to take all her clothes off before getting out of the car, and then to run naked into the house. The wife obliged her husband once, but his urgings on repeated occasions upset and worried her, and she was realistically concerned about the neighbors' seeing her. The husband wanted intercourse afterward as soon as he got into the house. He was definitely a voyeur who received sexual stimulation in this way.

What about the husband who wants his wife to dress in black undergarments, black stockings, or garters, and to do a provocative dance in front of him? Certainly he is probably not abnormal. If the wife is somewhat of an exhibitionist, she might even enjoy it, on occasion. But if she objects, as many wives would, insistence would be demeaning and humiliating, and show a calloused lack of consideration and respect for her feelings. Furthermore, many husbands would not ask this of their wives. The line between normal and deviant behavior is not always clearly drawn, but couples who love each other do try to be sensitive to each other's feelings, regardless of labels put on behavior. Continued insistence on unacceptable voyeuristic activities is an indication of unresolved conflicts and problems.

Troilism. One variation of voyeurism is *troilism*. This is the practice of sharing one's mate with another person so that one can look on. Or it can involve two couples having sexual intercourse in the presence of each other. This deviation is really a type of voyeurism and exhibitionism, or may be a manifestation of disguised homosexuality. In any case, it is more prevalent among men than women, and certainly ought to be considered deviant behavior.

Others. There are many other types of sexual deviations. Two of the most commonly known and most serious are *sadism* and *masochism*. Sadism is an abnormality in which a disturbed person gains sexual pleasure from inflicting psychological or physical pain on another person. Masochism is the condition in which a disturbed person receives sexual pleasure or gratification from being hurt, mentally or physically, by a sexual partner. *Nymphomania* is commonly discussed, but actually quite rare. It refers to the behavior of women who have an uncontrollable sexual desire that appears unquenchable, that they seek to fulfill regardless of the consequences. The term is often misused to refer to women with a high sexual drive, but nymphomaniacs are actually frigid women, incapable of orgasm, which is one reason they repeatedly seek sexual outlets. The male equivalent of nymphomania is *satyriasis,* which is an exaggerated desire for sexual gratification.

Several less common sexual deviations might be mentioned. *Mysophilia, coprophilia,* and *urophilia* are deviations in which individuals have an obsessive interest in excretory processes. *Saliromania* is a sexual disorder found primarily in men. It is characterized by a desire to damage or soil the body or clothes of a woman or a representation of a woman. The male who disfigures a statue or a painting of a woman often suffers from this illness. *Necrophilia* is a very uncommon deviation characterized by a desire to have sexual intercourse with a dead person.

One type of sexual deviation that arouses considerable anger and anxieties in communities is *pedophilia,* or "child molestation," in which adults seek sexual stimulation and gratification with children. Of all the sexual deviates, the child molester ranks next to the *rapists* as one of the most feared and despised.

Treatment. When the husband or the wife suspects marked sexual deviations in the other, psychological or psychiatric evaluation should be sought as the most appropriate response. Such evaluation will uncover the seriousness of the deviance, as well as recommend appropriate action. To some people, many very common types of sexual activity are abnormal. But to most people, the deviations described in this chapter are cause for concern. Some extreme sexual deviations are indications that the people who give evidence of them are very sick people. The right kind of help is needed. The last chapter of this book gives more detail about where to get help.

10

PROBLEMS OVER ADULTERY

ADULTERY AS A PROBLEM

Incidence and Seriousness. According to Dr. Frederick G. Humphrey, president of the American Association of Marriage and Family Counselors, nearly half of the cases brought to marriage counselors involve adultery. This statement was made by Humphrey (April 1977) on the basis of a survey of 100 marriage counselors across the country. (Humphrey, 1977) The situation is a particularly serious one, since one third of the couples who have extramarital sex planned to divorce because of the affair. In almost half the cases, the affair had been in progress for more than six months before help was sought, about half eventually told their mate of their affair, and in the majority of cases broke off the affair before seeking professional help. One in five of the wives, however, kept their affair going even after their spouse knew about it. Only 8 percent of the men did so. This difference may be because the women didn't get involved in extramarital affairs as easily as men, but when they did, they were more apt than men to be deeply involved emotionally. Humphrey found that the average couple had been married twelve years, were middle-class, and had at least one child. (Humphrey, 1977)

It's difficult to estimate the incidence of adultery in the general population. One study of 100 middle-class, middle-aged couples from two suburban areas of a large metropolitan city in the Midwest showed that 28 percent of these marriages had been affected by at least one instance of adultery.

Effects. When it happens, adultery affects couples in a variety of ways. Some marriages are never the same. The offended spouse can neither forget nor forgive. He or she finds it difficult to have intercourse afterward, because of thoughts of his or her spouse in bed with another person. If intercourse is permitted after the adultery is discovered, orgasm or enjoyment is difficult because the mind fantasizes what was happening when one's mate had sex with someone else.

Sometimes, of course, the offender, out of guilt, shame, or anxiety, becomes sexually unresponsive. He or she can't forget what has happened, and these thoughts prevent complete enjoyment.

Many times adultery takes place repeatedly over a period of time. But whether it is only a single incident or repeated behavior, it usually affects not only a couple's sexual life but their larger relationship: their feelings of love, trust, loyalty, commitment, and care. For a time at least, love is replaced by anger and resentment. Trust is replaced by distrust, fear, and doubt. Loyalty wanes because of the hurt and bitterness of being deceived. Since the offender has broken the pledge of faithfulness, the spouse's deep sense of loyalty is shattered. Commitment is replaced by cynicism or indifference. The desires to care for the other, and to be cared for, are repressed. One has been betrayed, one cannot let oneself care in the same way, nor trust that the other will do so again. Adultery creates emotional and psychological barriers between couples that are difficult to heal.

Of course, many couples do heal the rift, depending on the remorse and repentance of the offender and on the ability of the other to forgive. Trust, love, commitment, care—all can be restored—especially if the incident isn't repeated and if the couple are strongly motivated to make up and to save their love and marriage.

At the opposite extreme, of course, are those marriages which are not affected at all. One of the spouses is having an affair, but the other doesn't care. These are marriages in which the spiritual and emotional bonds between the couple are already broken, so the adulterous relationship is just evidence of the fractured marriage. When people don't really care, their marriage has become a utilitarian marriage of convenience. They stay together for financial reasons, practical reasons of convenience, for business reasons, even "for the sake of the children," but not because they love each other. For this reason, they are not really hurt or upset by the incident; rather, they are worried that the children will find out, or that friends and associates will know, and that they will be embarrassed.

In a study of upper-middle-class Americans reported in the book *The Significant Americans,* John Cuber quotes a husband who admits the deep pretense that he has built into his life for, as he says, "the sake of the children."

> We married on the basis of a few days' courtship and probably didn't make the best choice. I'm forty and still feel a strong urge when I see a young and attractive woman—and I've acted on it now and then—but (through clenched teeth and with a doubled fist) my wife and I agree on one thing—we've told each other that we would never get a divorce, on account of the children. They must never know—never. (Cuber, 1965, p. 41)

In between those couples who care deeply and those who do not care at all are those who say they love and care for each other and wouldn't think of breaking up their marriage but who still want to sleep with someone else. Very often, these persons see nothing wrong with extramarital relationships. Many of them had multiple partners before marriage and simply continue their sexual promiscuity after marriage. The biggest dilemma of these persons is how to keep their mate from finding out. They never tell of their affairs, and make every effort to keep them clandestine and deceive their mate. This attitude is represented by the remarks of one wife.

> I run around some, mostly when my husband is away on business trips, but I wouldn't think of telling him. He would be terribly hurt and upset. There's no way I could ever make him understand. So as far as I'm concerned, I love him and hope he never finds out.

The theory of this philosophy is that what others don't know won't hurt them. Thus, according to this philosophy, a husband feels he can have escapades as long as they are discreet and don't embarrass his wife, children, or boss. In some cases, a wife or a husband has found out, but pretends not to know, because to admit that one's spouse has been unfaithful is to risk a confrontation.

ALTERNATIVE LIFE-STYLES AND CONSENSUAL ADULTERY

Because of this hypocrisy and deceit, some persons have gone so far as to suggest *consensual adultery,* which is extramarital sexual intercourse with the full knowledge and consent of one's spouse. The theory is: if couples are honest and aboveboard, they aren't really creating distrust or destroying love; they are showing concern, respect, and consideration for each other, but are still being realistic and honest about their desire for sex with other persons. One author asks: "How appropriate is the word unfaithfulness in describing a sexual relationship of which the spouse knows and approves?" (Clayton, 1973, p. 97) Some persons look with disdain on those who practice *ambiguous adultery* (in which the spouse knows but does not fully approve) or *clandestine adultery* (in which the adultery is kept secret), and seek to promote their concept of consensual adultery.

This type of adultery is promoted under various arrangements: *open marriage, comarital* (rather than extramarital) *sex, swinging, group marriage,* and in some forms of *commu-*

nal living. All these variations are destructive to loving, monogamous marriage, as we shall see.

Open Marriage. The chief exponents of the concept of *open marriage* are George and Nena O'Neill in their book *Open Marriage.* (O'Neill and O'Neill, 1972) The O'Neills have many helpful things to say about marriage: the need for communication, flexible roles, companionship, equality, self-identity, trust, and love and sex without jealousy. These are important qualities in any marriage. But they also talk about what they call the fidelity trap, the unrealistic expectations of monogamy, and the need for shared companionships and open love. They write:

> In an open marriage, in which each partner is secure in his own identity and trusts in the other, new possibilities for additional relationships exist, and open (as opposed to limited) love can expand to include others. . . . In open marriage, you can come to know, enjoy and share companionship with others of the opposite sex besides your mate. . . .
>
> These outside relationships may, of course, include sex. That is completely up to the partners involved. If partners in an open marriage do have outside sexual relationships, it is on the basis of their own internal relationships, that is, because they have experienced mature love, have real trust, are able to expand themselves, to love and enjoy others and to bring that love and pleasure back into their marriage without jealousy. (O'Neill and O'Neill, 1972, pp. 253–254)

There are several strenuous objections to the O'Neills' point of view. One, they state that "sexual fidelity is the false god of closed marriage," that since fidelity involves duty or obligation, those who believe in it have eliminated possibilities of growth and sharing in their relationship. They write: "Fidelity in the closed marriage is the measure of *limited* love, *diminished* growth, and *conditional* trust." (O'Neill and O'Neill, 1972, p. 253) This, of course, is nonsense. Why should being lovingly faithful to one's mate preclude the possibility of growth? They also tend to make monogamy and fidelity synonymous with closed marriage, which they say includes deception, smothering togetherness, rigid role prescription, subjugation, unequal status, bondage, possession of the other, degeneration, and other strong adjectives. This kind of bigoted assumption simply doesn't hold true for thousands of couples whose monogamous marriages strongly testify to the fallacy of these assumptions.

Another strong objection is the fact that the O'Neills imply that anyone who has not been able to eliminate jealousy when one's mate is dating or sleeping with someone else has really not achieved maturity. They write:

> The idea of sexually exclusive monogamy and possession of another breeds dependencies, infantile and childish emotions, and insecurity. The more insecure you are, the more you will be jealous. . . . It is the fear of a loss of love. . . . It is . . . a serious impediment, then, to the development of security and identity. (O'Neill and O'Neill, 1972, p. 237)

Their whole argument is that jealousy is not instinctive; it is a learned response; people are not naturally monogamous: to be so is to deny one's nature.

Here again, the argument just doesn't agree with the facts. Jealousy is one of the most universal phenomena present in almost all cultures. Furthermore, polygamous societies are in the great minority, and down through the ages polygamy could exist without difficulty only when there were no affectional, romantic feelings between couples, where women were considered subservient to men: things and not persons. It is my conviction that in our culture the only persons who are not jealous are those who don't care for each other or who aren't worried that their mate really cares for someone else. As soon as a person's partner starts expressing an emotional interest in another jealousy arises. Is this bad? No, it is based upon real and not imagined threats. It serves a useful function in helping to protect the relationship.

And three, the O'Neills encourage sex without real feeling or love. They write: "The idea that sex without love is destructive, alienating, and unpleasurable is a purely cultural evaluation much akin to the idea that sex is dirty." (O'Neill and O'Neill, 1972, p. 249) They go on to admit, however, that "sex with love is best," and that without love it "may not be as rewarding, fulfilling or rich an experience as sex with love" (p. 249). If sex with love is best, then why cheapen it and settle for a superficial experience? Why risk losing one's real love for a meaningless encounter for the sake of physical pleasure? My thesis still holds: "Only within the context of a deep, committed, loving relationship is sex most meaningful and fulfilling to human beings."

Comarital Sex. The term *comarital sex* is really synonymous with consensual adultery. It is sexual intimacy with an extramarital partner to which a monogamous heterosexual couple openly agree prior to the involvement. It is with the knowledge and consent, but not necessarily the presence and participation of each member. Comarital sex is an internal part of the marriage arrangement rather than something external to it. It includes internal concurrence and negotiation rather than external collusion and deception. Hence, from this viewpoint, it is not considered extra.

Swinging. Comarital sex that includes an exchange of partners by married persons for sexual purposes and that does not include any emotional involvement at all is "recreational sex" and is commonly referred to as *swinging* or *mate-swapping*. Its chief characteristic is lack of emotional involvement.

There is really no reliable estimate of the numbers of couples who have been involved in swinging. Limited information reveals percentages of from 1.7 to as high as 5, but most of these samples are college-educated, upper-middle-class couples, so the figures obtained are probably high.

Typically, the husband more often than the wife initiates

the involvement. Negative reactions and revulsion by the wife stimulate the husband to begin convincing, or coercing, his wife to agree. The husband may invite a swinging couple in for a chat. If the husband is successful, the wife becomes resigned to trying out swinging. All wives and most husbands in one study approached their first experience with anxiety. (Varni, 1973) If nothing traumatic happens because of the initial sexual encounter, the couple are persuaded to try again. After the wives went through a period of conflict, some began to look forward to swinging with enthusiasm, sometimes to an even greater extent than their husbands. In some cases, the husbands began to worry, and tried to discontinue the activity.

What about the effect of swinging on marriage? One study that compared swinging couples with other couples showed that 49 percent of swinging husbands and 34 percent of swinging wives had been divorced and remarried, as compared with only 15 percent and 14 percent of the other husbands and wives. (Gilmartin and Kusisto, 1973) The chief reason for the breakup of the prior marriages was swinging.

A large number of couples who try swinging give it up, encountering quite difficult problems. A survey of 473 marriage counselors who were counseling swinging-dropout couples revealed that the most important reason for dropping out were, in decreasing order of importance: jealousy, guilt, threatening marriage, development of emotional attachment with other partner, boredom and loss of interest, disappointment, divorce or separation, wife's inability to "take it," fear of discovery (children or community), or impotence of the husband. (Denfeld, 1974) As can be seen, jealousy and guilt were the major reasons for couples' dropping out. Husbands reported more jealousy than wives. A number of husbands became concerned about their wife's popularity or sexual endurance capabilities (which were greater than theirs). A number of wives dropped out because they were fearful of losing their mate. Dropout couples reported that swinging weakened rather than strengthened their marriage. Fighting and hostility were frequent after swinging. In some cases, development of an attachment to swinging partners led to divorce and/or new marriages. In some cases, lying, cheating, and clandestine meetings were discovered which were in violation of swinger's rules. (Denfeld, 1974, p. 264)

Although this type of activity was supposed to be voluntary, some wives were forced into swinging for their husband's benefit. Once involved, a small percentage of husbands found themselves impotent. Fear of discovery by the children or the community were strong motives for dropping out.

In this same survey, when the counselors were asked to comment on couples who were still active swingers, the report was that these couples had the same problems as the dropouts, but more fear of discovery, venereal disease, and rejection.

One of the justifications that couples give for swinging is that it enriches their marriage. The facts do not support this rationalization. Many couples with an otherwise fairly average marriage have their relationship wrecked through this kind of activity. A sick marriage becomes even sicker. All couples face tremendous problems, which become increasingly difficult to deal with. Couples are caught in a dilemma. To keep from affecting their present marriage, they strive to keep from becoming emotionally involved with the other couples. If they are successful, their sexual relationship remains shallow and without emotional content. No matter how hard they try, guilt, fear, jealousy, and disgust arise, minimizing whatever pleasure they hoped to derive from the experience. The results of these experiences substantiate the conclusion: that it is almost impossible for most couples to be involved in ongoing adulterous, comarital sexual activities and to maintain a loving, trusting, fulfilling marriage at the same time. The couples are forced either to give up their adulterous relationship or to give up their marriage. Most find it extremely difficult to maintain both.

Group Marriage. *Group marriage* is at least four people, two
female and two male, in which each partner is "married" to
all partners of the opposite sex. (Constantine and Constantine, 1973) Usually, only two couples are involved; occasionally group marriage includes six persons. The Constantines
also refer to *multilateral marriage,* which may involve single
persons also. Triads, with either two men and one woman or
two women and one man, are common. We shall focus discussion here primarily on married couples within the larger
group. Thus, the group marriage includes couples who are
pair-bonded as well as those legally married. All such relationships involve sexual intimacy. In many cases, couples also
have children living with them. In the Constantines' study,
they worked with 26 groups, consisting of 104 adults and 56
children.

One of the first questions is: What motivates couples to try
out this type of arrangement? Couples list the following reasons as important: personal fulfillment, need for companionship, love for the other persons, opportunity for personal
growth, personality enrichment, benefits to children, sense
of community, variety of sexual partners, financial advantages, greater intellectual variety. In some cases, couples
enter group marriage as a means of trying to strengthen their
own relationship. If this is the motive, things usually get
worse, not better.

Typical was the case of Eleanor who felt her marriage to
Malcom did not give her the security she desired. Apparently, she felt that two partially committed husbands were
better than one. Actually, the group heightened her sense
of insecurity when she saw Malcom become deeply involved with the other woman and realized her own lack of
involvement with either the other man or woman. The
result for Eleanor was painful, and her jealousy added to
the frictions and tensions of the group. (Constantine and
Constantine, 1973, p. 1110)

As a result of these kinds of complications, the Constantines definitely do not recommend group marriage as a way of solving marital problems or as an alternative to divorce.

One of the noticeable features of group marriage is the continual efforts that couples must make to avoid jealousies and hurt feelings, and to avoid admitting that they develop preferential emotional and sexual attachments. The most common arrangement is to set up a fixed standard of rotation of partners, allotting three to four days with each partner. The theory is that fixed rotation eliminates decision-making and minimizes the problems mentioned. In spite of these efforts, jealousies and preferences arise. Jane becomes so devoted to Harold that she wants to have sex with him only. Bob may be perfectly potent with Helen, but not with Jane or Mary. Mary may be the least attractive of the females and play nasty tricks on the other girls because she thinks they are prettier than she. Matt may become disenchanted with all the females, and seeks adulterous affairs outside the group. The more persons involved, the more complex the interpersonal relationships become, and the more problems of sex, jealousy, and love arise. Multiple sexual encounters often stimulate fears, anger and rage, or despondency. Eighty percent of the couples in the Constantines' study reported that jealousy was a problem. (Constantine and Constantine, 1973)

Of course, many other types of problems arise: differences over personal and housekeeping habits, financial squabbles, problems with child-rearing. In an effort to work out problems, couples are forced to require rigid structure and rules. Sign-up sheets and rotational systems for baby-sitting and doing housework are common. Usually, group meetings must be held to elect a manager and a treasurer, to formulate plans, etc. The larger the group marriage, the more complicated the relationships become. One of the most frequent complaints of the children is, "Too many adults bossing us around and telling us what to do." In actual practice, the Constantines found that most groups broke up eventually, with a median duration of sixteen months. This indicates the inherent instability of this type of marital arrangement.

Communal Living. Communes are a further extension of group living arrangements, except that members do not strive to be "married" to all other members. Communes may include legally married, committed, monogamous couples as well as single persons. Some communes encourage "free love"; others positively forbid it. Some communes are highly structured, others are more open and flexible. Some have a religious orientation, others are nonsectarian. Some are urban, others are rural. The least successful communes are the nonstructured *utopian communes,* with a dropout orientation and a "do your own thing" philosophy. When work and management are not organized, the work does not get done, all kinds of problems remain unsolved, the communes break up. The most highly successful communes are the *religious communes:* highly structured, with an authoritarian leader and a work ethic. They are family oriented—that is, regular family groups exist and live within the larger structure. The most successful types of urban communes are *evolutionary* in character: made up of professional people, with straight jobs, who have no intention of giving up their middle-class comforts but who desire person-to-person intimacy in a communal setting. Their motive is often sexual variety, or the desire to pool resources for financial reasons, and to provide care for their children. However, many of these persons participate only on weekends, or as visitors, and so do not make a complete commitment to communal living. Generally speaking, the problems of communal living are the same as with any number of persons trying to get along together. Jealousies, misunderstandings, resentments, conflicts arise. Some groups never solve them and others are able to deal with them over a period of time through structure, organization, and rules. Thus, the problems that the individual married couple or family face are multiplied as additional persons become a part of the extended family. (Kanter, 1972)

CONCLUSIONS

Married people get into adulterous relationships for many
different reasons. Some persons get involved contrary to
their own inclinations and moral principles; they are sorry
and repentant and often never become involved again.
Often, however, their own guilt and the feelings of their
spouse are such as to destroy their affectionate relationship
or to break up their marriage. At other times, the rift is
healed. Other persons seek adulterous relationships because
of a defective marriage. They and their spouse have ceased
to care, but stay together in a utilitarian marriage for a variety of reasons. Still other "Bohemian" persons seek adulterous relationships as an expression of their own philosophy, as
an extension of their life-style. Most often, even if adultery
is by consent, couples find that it creates problems for them,
and so is not a way to strengthen marriage.

Whether adultery is accidental or intentional, clandestine,
ambiguous, or consensual, the overwhelming evidence is
that it is harmful to truly meaningful, loving, committed,
monogamous marriage. "Thou shalt not commit adultery" is
not only moral but necessary if monogamous marriage is to
survive.

PART III

MALE
SEXUAL DYSFUNCTION

11

PREMATURE EJACULATION

THE PROBLEM

Explanation. *Premature ejaculation was defined in Chapter 2 as the inability to delay ejaculation so the husband can place his penis within the vagina and continue intercourse and thrusting long enough for his wife to have orgasm 50 percent of the time.* This definition assumes that the wife can have an orgasm, and when she doesn't, it is because of the rapidity with which the husband ejaculates.

There have been efforts on the part of some sex therapists to give a more quantitative definition. One textbook defines premature ejaculation as one that takes place 30 seconds after intromission. Another says 1½ to 2 minutes; another says premature is any time before 10 thrusts. These definitions are too arbitrary, however, since rapidity of orgasm is quite variable with both men and women. For all practical purposes, a husband who usually takes one minute or so to have an orgasm, while his wife takes a longer time, may be ejaculating prematurely, at least as far as his wife is concerned. The net result—frustration—is the same as if he ejaculated in three minutes and she required four. Some husbands may ejaculate at the sight of the wife undressing; others after a few minutes of love play and prior to coitus itself; others immediately after the penis enters the vagina. Most premature ejaculators do so after intromission, and after several thrusts.

In all of these instances, however, the husband is unable to exert voluntary control over his ejaculatory reflex, so that once he is sexually aroused, he usually has an orgasm quickly. This is the important thing: he cannot exert control long enough to be able to have coitus for a sufficient length of time to bring his wife to climax. As a result, he is able to enjoy the sensations of intercourse only briefly, and, more important, his wife is not able to have an orgasm through coitus. By the time she begins to become excited and/or ready for orgasm, her husband has climaxed, loses his erection, and can't continue. Some husbands utilize manual stimulation of the clitoris to bring the wife to orgasm, and certainly this is preferred to no orgasm at all, but part of the enjoyment of intercourse is lost. One author insists that prematurity exists whenever there is an absence of voluntary control over the reflex, whether it occurs before the wife reaches orgasm or not.

Causes. There are a number of different causes of premature ejaculation. The cause may have originated in the husband's early sexual experience. A prostitute may have congratulated her client on his speedy performance because it meant she could go on to the next customer. A young man having intercourse in the car while parked may be worried about being caught in the act. Emphasis on speedy ejaculation as a desirable accomplishment may encourage the practice after a few episodes. Once the pattern is begun, it is difficult to change.

There are some males, also, who are either too selfish or too uninformed to try to bring their wife to orgasm. They either don't care or don't really know that the wife is supposed to have a climax too and that this takes time. Masters and Johnson found that these types of men are selfish and do not consider themselves inadequate lovers. In fact, they are proud of their quick orgasm, and blame their wife for not being sexy enough. (Masters and Johnson, 1970)

If antagonism or tension develops between the couple, and particularly if the husband is blamed by a critical wife and begins to feel anxious about his performance, his anxiety and resentment increase and further aggravate the condition. If he approaches coitus in a state of anxiety because he is fearful that he may not please his wife, his fear may be strong enough to motivate the husband to early ejaculation to relieve his anxiety. Either fear or anger toward one's partner, often a mixture of both, may cause prematurity.

There are various ways of expressing hostility—one way is in the bedroom. While clinical experience has not substantiated the hypothesis that premature ejaculators are universally hostile toward women, it has shown that they often are expressing hostility toward their own wife. Also, the husband who is very insecure, and overly concerned about his wife's responses, may be solving his conflict by orgasm as speedily as possible as a means of reassuring himself.

Effects. The long-term effects of continued premature ejaculation can be quite serious. The most immediate effect is the curtailment of the wife's enjoyment. Intercourse becomes completely male-oriented: providing the husband some pleasure but depriving the wife of sexual satisfaction. If a husband begins to avoid normal expression of affection or extensive love play to keep from getting excited, the wife may feel rejected and hurt by his "cold" behavior. If the husband and the wife can't talk about the situation, they are soon engaged in a vicious circle of hurt, anger, resentment, and avoidance, which destroys the possibility of sexual fulfillment. In their book *Understanding Human Sexual Inadequacy,* Belliveau and Richter write:

> When a man consistently ejaculates prematurely, the pattern of the marriage is somewhat predictable. At first, when the newlyweds discover that the husband cannot delay his ejaculation, they lovingly console each other and assure themselves that the situation will improve after they become accustomed to married life. Eventually many men do gain control, but millions do not.
> When the problem persists, the wife's attitude begins to

change. She starts to feel that she is being inconsiderately used, that her husband is concerned only with his own sexual needs. . . . Especially after stimulating foreplay, the wife is left with no means of release and a lot of resentment. (Belliveau and Richter, 1970, p. 112)

Quite typically, after a period of years the husband and the wife may become uninterested in the marriage, withdrawing from sexual encounter, the man either blaming his wife or doubting his own masculinity, and the wife either bitter toward the husband or losing confidence in herself as a woman. Sometimes the male becomes impotent, the mates unfaithful. If the marriage survives, it may become quite utilitarian, but without sex, often with much conflict. Many such marriages end in divorce.

Husbands react in one of two ways. The more selfish ones accept the situation as normal. They believe that sexual pleasure is a male prerogative and as long as they get pleasure from the experience that is all they care about. They remain unaware that giving as well as receiving enriches the total relationship.

Generally speaking, men of lower socioeconomic levels who are premature ejaculators rarely complain, even if the wife does. This attitude reveals a double standard: the wife is not supposed to have sexual feelings, she is regarded as a sexual receptacle to provide pleasure for the husband.

The second type of husband, usually of a higher socioeconomic level, is more considerate than the first type and becomes very upset over his ejaculatory incontinence. He regards it as a threat to his masculinity, and feels distressed that he is not able to satisfy his wife.

DO IT YOURSELF CURES

Usually the husband who is considerate wants to try to solve the difficulty. Like many other men, he may first employ "techniques" that he has read or heard about. These techniques usually involve efforts to try to distract himself to keep from getting excited so quickly. These techniques may include mental distractions such as thinking about something else during intercourse, counting backward from 100, thinking about business, or recalling a fishing trip. If these measures fail, which they often do, he tries physical distractions such as tensing his anal muscles, biting his lip, pinching himself, or pulling his hair. Perhaps he has read about creams or lotions that anesthetize the penis to prevent ejaculation, so he tries these. Some men use two or three condoms to try to cut down sensation. Other methods commonly tried are: masturbating to orgasm before intercourse to eliminate ejaculation during intercourse itself, having intercourse a second time to bring the wife to orgasm, having intercourse with the wife on top and the man below, which generally speeds the wife's orgasm and retards the husband's. Some men say they finish too fast when they're sober, so they take a couple of drinks to delay climax. The problem with this, however, is that one drink too many and the whole effort, literally, will collapse.

What are the results of some of these popular cures? Some of them work for some men—that is, they may delay ejaculation long enough for the wife to climax. In other instances, none of these work. However, each type of technique presents problems. Mental or physical distraction that tries to keep the man's mind off of sex attempts to prevent him from getting too excited. Such efforts, also, may completely prevent the wife from becoming aroused. She observes that her husband is trying to think of something else, that his mind is far off—thinking of business or a fishing trip. It's a little hard for him to concentrate on loving her and arousing her when he tries to keep his mind off of what he's doing. She wants him to be her lover—and this requires attention. As soon as his attention is focused on lovemaking, he ejaculates quickly. Some husbands come before love play even begins. Obviously, it takes more than distraction to cure that. The same principle holds true for physical distraction. It may work for a short time, then the pre-ejaculation occurs anyhow.

What about anesthetic types of creams or lotions? There may be some success, but there are also drawbacks. The "stay cream" must be applied some time before coitus to allow for the anesthetic to be effective. Then, it must be completely removed prior to coitus, or it will also have an anesthetic effect on the wife. The result is a pretty numb encounter. If it is removed too soon, however, the effect wears off. What about wearing several condoms? Certainly it prevents the penis from receiving very much physical stimulation through vaginal contact. But a large part of sexual arousal is mental: a condom won't help that. Neither will it help the man who ejaculates prior to intromission.

Masturbating prior to intercourse, or repeated coitus, may sometimes work. If a husband can maintain a second erection during coitus, without repeated orgasm right away, at least he can satisfy his wife. Some premature ejaculators, however, become impotent after their first orgasm, or such a long period has to expire that it takes too long until erectile capacity returns before coitus can be resumed. A few men are able to have repeated orgasms with the same problem of prematurity each time.

What about different positions during intercourse? For example, the wife on top and the husband below? This may help; however, few persistent problems are cured in this way.

The chief drawback with all of the above "remedies" is that they do not really assist the husband in obtaining ejaculatory control. They try to prevent him from getting too excited, but what is needed is some measure of control even under conditions of excitement. The more excitement and control, the more the husband and the wife both are able to enjoy intercourse. Who wants to make love without excitement? Under these circumstances, sex becomes too cold and impersonal.

THERAPEUTIC METHODS

Semans Method. There are two clinical methods which are used to help the premature ejaculator. One is the so-called *Semans method,* named for Dr. James Semans, who developed the technique in the 1950s. In this method, the wife is instructed to stimulate the husband's penis manually until he begins to approach orgasm. He then signals her to stop until his sexual excitement dies down. She then repeats the stimulation several times over, stopping each time in between to allow her husband's excitement to wane. Finally, the fourth time she masturbates him to orgasm.

During manual stimulation, the husband is encouraged to focus his attention on the erotic sensations he feels. He is also urged not to try to gain conscious control over orgasm, except that of signaling his wife when to stop. To do so would be to try to deny his erotic sensations, and that is just the opposite of what is desired. The more the husband is aware of his sensations and can delay climax, the more control is achieved. But control is obtained not by denial but by conscious focusing on the sensations and by interrupting physical stimulation before climax. After a number of these sessions over a period of days, the husband becomes more aware of improvement in orgastic control.

The next step is intercourse with the wife on top. She puts his penis into her vagina and stimulates with gentle thrusting until he asks her to stop. After they remain still for a while, the husband's excitement wanes. The wife again starts thrusting. This procedure is repeated until coitus proceeds to ejaculation the fourth time arousal occurs.

Once control is attained in the female superior position, the couple are instructed to have intercourse while lying on their side, using the stop and start method. When control is attained in this position, the couple are permitted to have intercourse with the husband superior, in which most men reach a climax most easily. This position is used only after a high degree of control is obtained.

Squeeze Technique. Masters and Johnson have adopted a variation of the Semans method which they call the *squeeze technique.* (Masters and Johnson, 1970) The wife stimulates her husband manually as before but just prior to orgasm, she holds the penis between her thumb and the first two fingers of one hand. The thumb is placed on the underneath side of the area where the head of the penis begins, and the two fingers are placed on the opposite side from the thumb, where the ridge separates the glans (head) from the shaft. The wife then squeezes hard for 3 to 4 seconds. The pressure causes the husband to lose the urge to ejaculate; he may also lose some of his erection. After 15 to 30 seconds, excitement dies, and the wife caresses her husband's penis to full erection once more, and again uses the squeeze technique to prevent ejaculation. This continues for 15 to 20 minutes without ejaculation. If this procedure is repeated for a period of days, the husband begins to learn some ejaculatory control. Usually the couple are much encouraged by the progress.

The next step is for the husband to lie flat on his back and the wife to straddle him. Before insertion, she is instructed to apply the squeeze technique two or three times. After intromission, the wife remains motionless so that her husband can get used to the feeling of penile containment and until his excitement subsides. If the husband feels he is going to ejaculate, the wife raises her body and repeats the squeeze procedure before reinserting the penis.

After a few days, the wife is instructed to thrust just enough to sustain her husband's erection. The couple now may find they can remain together for 15 to 20 minutes before ejaculation.

After control increases, the couple move from the female superior position to the lateral (side-by-side) position, and from there to the male superior position in which ejaculatory control is more difficult.

Many couples are able to achieve control in a matter of weeks, although complete ejaculatory control may take six to twelve months. Therapists instruct couples to use the squeeze technique once a week for the first six months and to practice it for 15 or 20 minutes at some time during the wife's menstrual period. Couples are also advised to rely on the squeeze technique after they have been apart from each other and sexual tensions are high. If the husband ever becomes temporarily impotent because the couple overdoes it, the couple are instructed not to use the squeeze method for a while, and to let potency return by itself.

12

IMPOTENCE

DESCRIPTION

Impotence is the inability to create and maintain an erection for a sufficient period of time to complete sexual intercourse satisfactorily. The condition may always have existed *(primary impotence),* so that the husband has never been able to maintain an erection quality sufficient to achieve a successful coital connection. This condition is not common, but is considered serious. In other cases *(secondary impotence)* there may have been numerous successful encounters before, but then repeated episodes of erective failure occur. If failure occurs in at least 25 percent of the attempts, a diagnosis of secondary impotence is made. Of course, many husbands experience occasional failure because of fatigue, illness, drinking, distraction, or other reasons, but this is not really secondary impotence because of its temporary nature. It has been estimated that approximately half of the male population has experienced occasional transient episodes of impotence, so this is to be considered normal. As such, it should not be taken seriously. The danger is that a husband will start to worry about it and develop enough anxiety to cause it to happen again. A man who becomes very sensitive about his loss of erection because he feels it is a reflection on his masculinity is creating problems for himself. He is more likely to experience erectile failure again, not because there is anything wrong with him, but because of his anxiety. Erectile problems occur in men of all ages, races, and socioeco-nomic levels: in the muscular teen-ager as well as in the senile senior citizen.

CAUSES

Diagnosis. The cause of impotence can be either physical or psychological, so unless the reason seems to be clearly situa-tional, every impotent male should have a complete medical and neurological checkup.

Sometimes it is not easy to determine whether the cause is physical or not. One simple test has been developed by Dr. Ismet Karacan, professor of psychiatry at Baylor College of Medicine in Houston. Patients are monitored while in their sleep to see if they have normal erections during the so-called REM (Rapid Eye Movement) periods of sleep, which occur every hour and a half and last from twenty to thirty minutes. If erections during these periods are normal, the cause is psychological. Men who are impotent for organic reasons have little or no swelling.

Two delicate pressure gauges are placed at the base and near the top of the penis to record any changes in diameter during the night. The results can be observed or registered on a strip of graph paper that reels out while the man is sleeping. Dr. Karacan says the patient can even test himself at home with a small portable unit. This erection test is the most useful of all those used to screen impotent patients.

Physical Causes. Two major categories of physical causes of sexual dysfunction have been discussed briefly in Chapter 3. Those causes are the use of certain *drugs* and specific *physical illnesses* or *debilitation*.

One of the major causes of secondary impotence is exces-sive use of *alcohol*. In quantities, alcohol is a sedative that has an inhibiting effect upon the transmission of nerve impulses, dulls erotic feelings and sensations, and decreases the possi-bility of sexual response. Under sedation, the vascular reflex mechanism fails to pump sufficient blood into the blood vessels and capillaries of the penis to render it firm and erect. Although a man intoxicated with alcohol may feel aroused and excited under sexual stimulation, his penis does not become erect.

In cases of severe and chronic alcoholism, the damage to the nerves may be permanent, not only because of the alcohol itself but because most alcoholics don't eat properly and suffer nutritional deficiencies. As a result, the neurological connections are damaged, so that the nerve impulses are not transmitted. If the disease is not too far advanced, vitamin therapy, high protein diet, and careful regulation of nutritional intake may restore some of the original functioning. Severely damaged nerve cells, however, are not repairable.

Males who are able to function sexually only under the influence of alcohol have a psychological problem, not a physical problem. They need alcohol to deaden anxieties, inhibitions, and fears so they are able to be more responsive. The problem with this, however, is that such persons may be on the road to alcoholism. It has become a crutch upon which they lean. In this case, there is a real danger of developing dependency. Of course, an overdose may prevent erection rather than enhance it.

The same principles hold true for drugs that are used as "mood elevators." These include the various sedatives (primarily *barbiturates*) and *tranquilizers* mentioned in Chapter 3. When used to treat anxiety or depression, they may increase potency, but when abused by being used in excess, they have an inhibiting effect. The same holds true for *amphetamines.* The effect of these stimulants on sexuality is closely dose related. In the usual recommended doses, there is no effect; medium doses are said to enhance orgasm sensations and decrease inhibitions, but high doses produce withdrawal symptoms within twenty-four hours, which include loss of interest in sex as well as in everything else. Men who use high doses of amphetamines go through two stages: at first they are able to maintain an erection for a long period of time but without being able to ejaculate, and next they lose erectile capacity.

There are a large number of other drugs that affect potency. The use and abuse of *narcotics* has a depressive effect on the central nervous system, and so is highly destructive to both sexual desire and potency. Other detrimental drugs are *anticholinergic* drugs, *antiadrenergic* drugs, *parasympathalytic* and *estrogenic* medication, *ACTH,* and *cortisone.* Men who are on any type of drug and have any problem at all with impotency ought to get medical help to determine if their problem is drug related.

A number of specific physical illnesses are causative factors in impotency. One of the most common of these is *diabetes.* Male diabetics often complain of loss of potency. The impotence may have started in the early, untreated stages of the disease. If the disease is treated promptly, potency may be restored by management of the diabetes. This is why many physicians prefer to include fasting blood sugar and glucose tolerance tests as part of a routine examination for potency problems. However, once impotency has become firmly established, management of the diabetes does not restore erectile security. The reason now is psychological. The male has begun to have fears of performance, and these fears become a part of his daily life and are now the controlling factor in the secondary impotence. Thus, for the impotent male who has had diabetes for some time before it was treated, correcting the condition must go beyond help for the diabetes and include elimination of the psychological causes of the problem.

Another physical illness in impotence is *arteriosclerosis.* In this disease, lesions within certain arteries obstruct the blood supply, causing limping in both legs and impotence. Usually this is associated with pain in the hip or legs. Surgical correction of the arteriosclerotic lesions can frequently restore a man to full potency.

Operations for *disease of the prostate glands* sometimes cause impotence. However, it is rarely the result of organic factors. Dr. Richard Ehrlich writes:

Psychiatric studies have shown that impotence is more often a result of multiple emotional as opposed to organic difficulties.

In a man widowed at an early age, preoccupation with a premature decline or loss of potency coupled with demands of dating and sexually satisfying new and younger partners no doubt produces anxiety and fear of performance. The need to assign this . . . to an organic basis often is a subconscious escape mechanism. Despite multiple regimens employed by urologists to cure impotence supposedly caused by prostatic difficulties, the best chances for improvement are obtained with psychiatric treatment. (Ehrlich, 1975, p. 93)

In *Parkinson's disease,* impotence usually is the result of advanced organic involvement. In this case, there is very little psychological component to impotence, as indicated by the fact that the impotence sometimes responds to the administration of special drugs. *Infectious hepatitis* also is a common cause of impotence. Another category of medical problems includes any and all resulting in a *low androgen level* in the bloodstream, which affects both sexual drive and potency. General *physical debilitation, fatigue,* or *nutritional deficiencies* can also cause impotency.

Psychological Causes. By far the greater number of causes of impotence are psychogenic—that is, they involve psychological and emotional factors. Men who are sensitive and emotionally vulnerable may react with acute anxiety whenever faced with frustrations, upset, or stress. This anxiety disrupts the delicate physiological balance of the erectile response and precipitates impotence. What are some of the most common sources of stress that causes impotence?

One of the most common is fear of failure. A man who feels pressured to perform, and is anxious about his ability to satisfy, may be under enough stress to cause impotence—which unconsciously becomes his defense against the demands of his wife. Even when fear of failure is not the primary cause of impotence, an incident of erectile insufficiency may trigger fears that subsequently become the causal factors in the problem.

The recent emphasis on the "liberated woman" who is sexually potent, multiorgasmic, and has high expectations and demands for sexual performance can have a negative effect on the man's sexual response. When asked by her counselor how often she would like to have intercourse, one wife replied: "At least twice each night." The husband sat in numb silence, incredulous, but also fearful. He was a man in his fifties and, I'm sure, completely skeptical of his ability to fulfill such requirements. Some women are quite demanding sexually, not because they really need that much sex, but because of the emotional need for reassurance of their desirableness, and because of the need for affection and love. Husbands who recognize that the real need is emotional, not just sexual, may be able to satisfy them through ordinary expressions of affection in addition to sexual intercourse.

The more demands are placed upon the husband, the more resistant he is likely to become, and the more his emotional reaction tends to impair his sexual response. The whole approach in treatment is to encourage pleasuring without the demand for performance. Once the pressure is off and anxiety diminished, erectile sufficiency can be restored. Men who are insecure about their masculinity may remain potent as long as they feel they are in psychological control and in charge of the situation, but if pressured by the female who shows too much aggressiveness, they begin to develop fear and anxiety about the loss of their masculinity and their erection.

Another cause of impotency is ambivalence about the person, the relationship, or the encounter. If a man feels disgusted, guilty, ashamed, or has other negative feelings about his sex partner, or about having intercourse with her, his anxiety may result in impotence. Such experiences are common in encounters with prostitutes. A young man whose first sexual encounter is with a prostitute may be completely disgusted and humiliated by the experience. The squalid room, the repelling physical appearance of the woman, her degrading approach, may make sexual arousal impossible. If the prostitute is amused and derides him, she may destroy his self-confidence. Some such men have become primarily impotent as a result of the trauma of this initial encounter, unable to have intercourse with other women because it has become a degrading experience in their eyes, and one to be avoided.

Married men who become involved in adulterous relationships, but who feel guilty and ashamed, may find themselves impotent with their extramarital partner. Sometimes, of course, the reverse is true. A husband who has a disturbed, hostile relationship with his wife and who is impotent with her may find himself potent with another woman, particularly if she seems sensitive and caring. It is not uncommon for a man to be impotent with one partner but not another.

Any type of traumatic sexual encounter early in life may cause impotency. Therapists occasionally see patients whose mothers have made sexual overtures: caressed them or masturbated them. Such encounters may be traumatic enough to cause impotency. The same is true of homosexual encounters. The following account was given by a college male.

> I left home when I was still in my teens, and got in with a group of older fellows who were homosexuals. I was young, and they thought handsome, and soon became the favorite of several of them. For the next several years, I lived with them and did everything they asked. But finally I couldn't take it any more. I became so disgusted I had to run away. I vowed to give up that kind of life. I met and asked out several girls, but each time one of them made advances, I knew I couldn't have intercourse with her. I felt I would never make it.

This young man had become so disgusted with his earlier homosexual experiences that he became fearful he could never respond as a normal male. He did write a year later, however, that he had met a girl whom he loved very much and was overjoyed to discover that he was potent with her. Sex, for him, had lost some of its negative associations and he was finally able to respond in a loving relationship.

Sometimes, the husband-wife relationship becomes so hostile and disturbed that the husband loses all desire and capacity for intercourse. The following account was given by one counselor.

A forty-nine-year-old male came to my clinic for treatment of impotence. His wife reported he had protracted nocturnal erections. When she discovered his erection, she would quickly mount him, only to awaken him. As soon as he woke up, his erection would quickly subside. Discussion revealed a deep-seated hostility between the couple. His wife was furious at him for his impotence, and took every opportunity to humiliate him verbally. The husband reported withdrawing from the relationship, but his bitter resentment erupted in a violent argument whenever his wife's sharp tongue became unbearable. Psychologically, his resentment was expressed in his withholding himself sexually from her.

In Chapters 3 and 6 reference was made to *the effects of negative, repressive, sex education on sexual responsiveness.* Masters and Johnson found that the single most common factor in the backgrounds of sexually dysfunctional people was rigid adherence to religious restrictions. They treated a number of primarily impotent men from families that demanded unquestioning obedience to religious rules. Taboos and misinformation doomed them to erective failure. Unfortunately, the men chose wives with equally restrictive religious backgrounds. Five of these women suffered from severe vaginismus. (Belliveau and Richter, 1970, p. 132) Fortunately, modern-day church teachings are now contributing in a positive way to the development of wholesome attitudes and feelings about sex, and this contributes to satisfying sexual relations in marriage.

Upsetting events or circumstances that stimulate a great deal of anxiety may trigger impotency. Dr. Barrie Greiff writes:

> A forty-year-old male has neglected his attractive and very understanding wife for several months after losing a promotion to a junior colleague. I have examined him at his wife's insistence, but find no other contributing factors, either in the marriage or his physical condition. The interview suggests that he now has fears of failing sexually and avoids the possibility. (Greiff, 1975, p. 92)

The author goes on to suggest that extremely competitive, ambitious men who are deeply committed to their work are more likely to become severely depressed when anticipated promotions are not forthcoming. This man had a deep sense of failure, reduced self-confidence, and doubts about his masculine image. He could not face his wife. He was depressed and upset. His emotional upset caused a temporary alteration in his sexual functioning.

Persons who show symptoms of depression—insomnia, loss of appetite, disinterest in what is going on around, frequent crying and disturbance, or other manifestations of upset—may also show loss of sexual drive and potency. Proper treatment for the depression will usually restore the potency.

TREATMENT

Five Approaches. There are essentially five basic approaches to the treatment of impotence.

1. *Medical approaches,* which seek to uncover and to correct physical conditions that are the cause of impotence. It is suggested that possible physical causes be checked out before it is assumed that the problem is psychological.

2. *Hormonal approaches,* using the male hormone testosterone.

3. *Psychoanalysis and psychotherapy,* to deal with deep-seated anxieties, conflicts, and phobias. This approach at-

tempts to reconstruct the patient's personality by fostering resolution of his unconscious conflicts. It is based on the assumption that sexual problems are an outgrowth of emotional difficulties.

4. *Marital therapy and counseling,* to deal with destructive interactions between the couple. It strives to improve the quality of the couple's total relationship, so that they can function more adequately sexually.

5. *Symptom-focused sex therapy,* concerned with sexual functioning and the relief of the person's sexual symptoms. In doing this, it uses sexual and erotic tasks which the couple do at home. It systematically structures these tasks, and these, combined with conjoint (couple together) therapy, are the means for correcting the dysfunctions.

The Use of Testosterone. At one time, physicians administered testosterone as the "cure-all" for male sexual dysfunction. Its use declined as physicians discovered that it was not always effective and that many impotent males had no testosterone deficiencies. Psychiatrists also began to emphasize the role of emotional factors in the disorder.

Recent evidence suggests, however, that testosterone may play a helpful role in the treatment of impotence in some cases. A series of studies of thousands of men with erectile problems due to either hormonal deficiencies or psychological causes showed that the administration of a drug that contained testosterone and other substances facilitated both erection and orgasm in 60 to 90 percent of patients with psychogenic impotence. (Kaplan, 1974, p. 274) Moreover, in many patients, potency persisted for an indefinite period of time after discontinuance of the drug. Of course, the drug may also have had a positive psychological effect, giving the patient encouragement and hope. But the fact remains that it did increase sexual drive and enhance response. It is sometimes prescribed when sexual drive seems to be weak.

Physicians warn, however, that it is most helpful in cases of demonstrable androgen deficiency. It is not used if there has been any history of prostatic cancer. Prolonged use can result in sodium retention and edema, and a depression of sperm count, although these are reversible after the medication is stopped. Certainly, part of the benefit is psychological. The most beneficial results are obtained from a combination of hormonal and sex therapy.

Psychoanalysis and Psychotherapy. Psychoanalysis and psychotherapy are most helpful when impotence is due to deep-seated conflicts and anxieties which must be resolved if the man is to function sexually. However, impotence is not invariably a manifestation of emotional problems or mental illness. It can occur in men who function well in other areas and have no psychological problems. In many cases, it has its roots in more immediate and simpler problems which can be dealt with through the symptom-focused methods of sex therapy. One comparison of the results of psychoanalysis and psychotherapy versus symptom-focused sex therapy showed that the former produced a 57 percent cure rate of impotence after two years of treatment, whereas the latter approach was effective in 74 percent of the cases treated for secondary impotence over a two-week period. (O'Connor and Stern, 1972) Psychoanalysis is expensive and time-consuming, and, overall, not as effective as sex therapy.

Symptom-focused Sex Therapy. This approach seeks to modify the specific factors that exert a direct and immediate effect on the man's erectile response. Thus, if a man has fear of sexual failure, if he suffers from guilt or conflict, or otherwise has difficulty expressing his sexual feelings, he and his wife are given sexual tasks to perform which help to remove the negative feelings and which show him that he is potent under nonstressful conditions.

Most therapists assign some nondemand "pleasuring" tasks to perform. (See Chapter 5, "Pleasuring and Lovemaking Techniques") In the beginning, the wife is instructed not to touch her husband's genitals, and coitus and ejaculation are prohibited for a period of days. Her teasing, enticing, gentle stimulation of other areas of her husband's body, without any concern about performance, helps to relax him and minimizes fears and other negative feelings. After a period of days, the genital areas are also stimulated. If it has not happened before, usually the husband begins to produce spontaneous erections during these pleasuring sessions. These demonstrate to him that he is potent.

If the husband is fearful that he will not be able to regain his erection, the squeeze method is used on his penis (see Chapter 11) until his erection subsides; then stimulation is resumed until the erection is restored.

The husband is instructed to try to eliminate all distracting thoughts, to engage in sexual fantasies that he finds stimulating, or to focus on his erotic sensations and not to worry about whether his erection is firm, whether it will go down, or whether or not his wife is enjoying it. The husband is instructed to be "selfish" to let his wife pleasure him, and not to be concerned with her reactions or thoughts for the time being.

After potency is restored through pleasuring, coitus is resumed. The wife stimulates her husband to have an erection, and lowers herself on him when his erection is firm. In the beginning, she separates without ejaculation. In later sessions, they may thrust to orgasm if they are inclined. The point is: at no time are the couple to feel that erection or orgasm is demanded.

Some psychotherapy is usually combined with sex therapy as a means of relieving anxieties, fears, and other negative feelings. If the marriage is quite disturbed, some marital therapy may be recommended. Usually, however, as the couple's sexual life improves, the marriage gets better also.

PROGNOSIS

When a husband who has secondary impotence is given proper help by competent therapists, the prognosis of improvement is quite favorable. The majority of patients are relieved of their erectile dysfunction after 2 to 10 weeks of treatment. Masters and Johnson were able to help 70 percent to erectile sufficiency. (Masters and Johnson, 1970) Primary erectile dysfunction has a less favorable prognosis, but Masters and Johnson still report a 60 percent cure rate. (Masters and Johnson, 1970) Once cured, none of these men suffered a relapse. After five years, 11 percent of those who had been treated for secondary impotence suffered a reversal.

13

EJACULATORY INCOMPETENCE

DESCRIPTION

Definition. *Ejaculatory incompetence is the inability of the male to ejaculate while his penis is in the vagina.* He becomes sexually excited, maintains an erection, and may be able to keep his penis in the vagina for thirty minutes to an hour, but does not have an orgasm during penile containment.

Degrees. There are various degrees of ejaculatory incompetence. In the most severe cases, the man has never had an orgasm, regardless of the method of stimulation. One such case is that of a nineteen-year-old man who is normally developed, who gets adequate erections, but who states that he has never had an emission either while masturbating or during intercourse. He also has never had a nocturnal emission. Such cases are actually very rare. Some men can have an orgasm while masturbating, but not during intercourse. In other cases, the husband can never ejaculate in the presence of his wife. He must leave the room to masturbate in order to gain relief from sexual tension. Some husbands have intercourse and masturbate afterward; others never copulate. Some must wait until the excitement of heterosexual contact dies down before they can reach a climax. Some husbands report that their ejaculatory reflex becomes inhibited by the mere touch of their partner.

More commonly, the husband can never reach an orgasm during intercourse, but is able to through manual or oral stimulation by his wife. He may try various schemes to achieve a climax: prolong coitus for up to an hour, use various forms of fantasy, have a drink ahead of time, or employ other techniques, but without success. However, if he withdraws and is masturbated by his wife, or if he does so in her presence, he climaxes easily. Some husbands can reach a climax only through fellatio.

It is not unusual for most men to have occasional episodes of ejaculatory failure. This happens more frequently in older men, especially if intercourse has been too frequent, or it happens occasionally to any husband during periods of fatigue, illness, distraction, or anxiety. This is not to be considered a problem, since ejaculation occurs at most other times.

Consequences. Most husbands and wives prefer that the husband have an orgasm during intercourse itself. Even though some wives are multi-orgasmic and can reach several orgasms during the long periods the husband can maintain an erection without ejaculation, it is a mistake to believe they are more satisfied than the wives whose husband comes after a normal period of time. Most wives are upset by their husband's ejaculatory incompetence. They are deprived of the pleasure of knowing that they have brought their husband to climax. After all, part of the satisfaction of intercourse is in the mutual exchange of pleasure. There is satisfaction in giving as well as receiving. These wives are wise enough to realize that intercourse without release is a frustrating experience for the husband. Some wives blame themselves; others feel (sometimes correctly) that the husband is holding back, that he can't give himself completely in intercourse. This realization hurts and prevents enjoyment. They interpret their husband's reaction as a personal rejection of them. As a result, some husbands pretend to have an orgasm while wearing a condom to prevent the wife from finding out about their disability, or because they don't want to disappoint her.

Sometimes, secondary impotence develops as a result of the inability to ejaculate. The husband's anticipation of failure and frustration is enough to block erection. Thus, the problem becomes compounded. He may start avoiding his wife and intercourse because of shame and fear. Naturally, the wife becomes even more frustrated, hurt, and rejected, and may react with anger or resentment, or by withdrawing from close contact. As in most serious problems of sexual dysfunction, if the problem goes on long enough, it usually has a quite negative effect on the total marital adjustment.

It is important, therefore, for the couple to try to remedy the situation.

CAUSES

There are a number of different causes. Most are psychological; occasionally the causes are physical. Thus, as in other problems of sexual dysfunction, if organic problems are suspected, these should be investigated first.

Physical. Among the specific organic conditions that can cause ejaculatory disturbances are the following:

1. *Depressed androgen (testosterone) level*—This has a depressive effect upon not only ejaculation but sexual drive and potency.

2. *Undetected diabetes*—Usually affects erection as well as ejaculation.

3. *Use of certain drugs*—Particularly antihypertensive, antipsychotic drugs, or antiadrenergic drugs. Since the sympathetic nervous system controls the emission phase of ejaculation, any drugs which act upon that nervous system may affect emissions. So-called "dry ejaculation," in which the man reaches an orgasm but without seminal emissions, has been reported.

4. *Debilitating illnesses*—especially those involving the nervous system.

Psychological. The most common causes of ejaculatory incompetence are psychological. When the man is in an aroused emotional state or when he suffers from a psychological conflict, he subconsciously "holds back," putting up an involuntary defense to avoid anxiety, thus inhibiting his ejaculatory reflex. In this case, he is overcontrolled, unable to release orgasm which is under the control of his brain.

One of the most common causes is fear of impregnating his wife. The husband is so afraid of getting his wife pregnant that either consciously or unconsciously he is unable to ejaculate. Use of an adequate birth control method in which the husband has confidence will do much to allay such fears.

Sometimes the problem originates with a single traumatic event. Masters and Johnson tell of one incident of a husband returning home to find his wife in bed with another man.

> The man had just ejaculated, and his semen was dripping from his wife's vagina. The couple remained married, but the husband was not able to ejaculate intravaginally again. He felt his wife's vagina was contaminated by the other man's semen. The thought of letting his semen mix with the other man's was repugnant, so that he could not ejaculate. (Masters and Johnson, 1970)

Boys who have been severely punished for masturbation, for soiling the sheets of their bed through nocturnal emissions, may have been so ashamed and upset by the experience that they are not able to experience orgasm in marriage later in life.

It is not uncommon in premarital or extramarital encounters for the man to find that he cannot reach an orgasm through ordinary intercourse. His anxiety and guilt prevent complete response.

> Mr. X. had always been able to have an orgasm while having intercourse with his wife. On one occasion he had intercourse with another woman, only to find, much to his surprise, that he could not come, even though he prolonged coital activity for over an hour.

One of the most important causes of ejaculatory incompetence is unresolved conflict or hostility toward the wife. The man who has not resolved his oedipal conflict, who feels incestuous while having intercourse with his mate, may not be able to have an orgasm with her, even though he might be able to with another woman. In instances where a great deal of hostility develops in the husband-wife relationship, withholding orgasm becomes a means of expressing that hostility. The man stops short of orgasm as a means of punishment. He doesn't want to give his wife the satisfaction of knowing that she can "control" him by arousing him to climax. His hostility makes him hold back, so he is never able to let himself go enough to ejaculate. In another case, a husband's fear of rejection prevents him from letting go. He doesn't want to be hurt, so he is inhibited.

It may be too that the husband finds his wife sexually repulsive, or that he simply doesn't get excited by her. One husband commented:

> I really wasn't in love with my wife when we married. I married her because of her money and social position and because my family wanted me to. We've been married over twenty years now. She's gotten careless and sloppy, I really don't find her exciting. I'm seldom able to have an orgasm with her through regular intercourse.

The husband with strong homosexual tendencies may be able to have a climax only with another man, not with his wife. He feels uneasy and anxious in her presence.

TREATMENT

Symptom-focused Treatment. Symptom-focused treatment of ejaculatory incompetence attempts to do two things. First, those specific factors which are inhibiting the man from ejaculating need to be identified. This is done through counseling sessions which explore feelings and increase the husband's insight into irrational fears, traumatic memories, or destructive interactions which are presently operating to reinforce his inhibitions. If the man becomes aware of the reasons for his inhibitions, and these can be brought out into the open and discussed, some of the negative feelings can be minimized and the man feel freer to express himself.

Second, symptom-focused treatment employs sexual tasks that the couple are instructed to perform. The purpose of these tasks is to decondition or extinguish the undesirable feelings and responses of the husband so that inhibiting responses no longer affect his capacity for orgasm. Gradually the husband is conditioned to respond sexually as the various tasks are performed in a step-by-step way.

Most therapists instruct the couple to begin with "pleasuring" sessions for the first few days. They may engage in any love play they find desirable, except that the husband is instructed not to ejaculate or enter the vagina. He may stimulate his wife to orgasm; the couple may engage in mutual manual or oral stimulation.

After several sessions of this nondemand pleasuring, erotic interest increases and sexual arousal becomes pronounced. At this point, the husband is given permission to ejaculate under circumstances where success is assured. If he can't ejaculate in the presence of his wife, she is instructed to arouse him to a high level of excitement, at which point he leaves her presence and masturbates to orgasm. This sets up an association between his wife's stimulation and his ejaculation. If he can masturbate in the presence of his wife, he is first stimulated by her; then he masturbates to orgasm in her presence. If he does this immediately after she has caressed him, this too develops a relationship between his orgasm and her stimulation.

If this is successful, the next step is for his wife to stimulate him to ejaculation manually or orally. If this is successful, the next stage is penile stimulation while the penis is close to the vagina. This time a lubricant such as petroleum jelly can be used, since this more closely approximates the feeling of penile-vaginal containment. Finally, the wife stimulates her husband to impending orgasm, at which time she mounts him in the female superior position and inserts his penis into her vagina, thrusting until ejaculation occurs. If her husband fails to ejaculate, the wife is instructed to slip the penis out and go back to manual stimulation. After she brings her husband close to ejaculation, she reinserts his penis and tries once more.

After ejaculation has occurred intravaginally, the husband is instructed to enter the vagina at a lower level of excitement, at which time the wife stimulates the penis to orgasm with her hand while the penis is inside her. Through this procedure, the husband is usually able to reach the stage where he can ejaculate normally inside the vagina, after the usual foreplay preceding intercourse. The couple are also instructed to prolong foreplay and ejaculation long enough for both the husband and the wife to have an orgasm with the penis in the vagina.

Results. Masters and Johnson were able to report success with 14 out of 17 men who were treated for ejaculatory incompetence. (Masters and Johnson, 1970) Other therapists report similar success.

The success of treatment depends upon several factors. One, success is obtained only by complete cooperation of both the husband and the wife. One advantage of conjoint therapy is that it encourages the husband and the wife to talk about the problem, to try to tackle the problem together, and to offer encouragement, love, and help to each other. Thus, a favorable climate for considerate marital interaction is encouraged.

Two, success in treatment of ejaculatory incompetence depends partially on its severity. Men who have very deep-seated anxieties and fears about vaginal ejaculation are harder to treat. Long-term psychotherapy may be needed, with success uncertain. Men who have never ejaculated intravaginally also have a poorer prognosis of success. If the problem is due to severe marital discord, the progress depends not only upon completion of the sexual tasks but upon the success of marital therapy itself.

14

LOW SEXUAL DRIVE

THE PROBLEM

Permanent Lack of Interest. An increasing number of wives are complaining about their husband's lack of interest in sexual relations. The following example is typical of these complaints:

> My husband and I are in our late thirties; we're both in good health as far as we know. We seem to get along pretty well except for one thing—my husband spends every night after supper watching television. He watches every program until at least 2 in the morning; sometimes I find him asleep in the chair, even after the station has signed off. I've asked him, even begged him, to come to bed early, but he never will. So I go to bed by myself. I'm all alone and feel rejected. I'd like my husband to make love to me, but he seldom does. It's getting so he doesn't seem interested more than once a month. What's the matter with him that he is so uninterested in sex? I'm reasonably attractive, and have a nice figure, but it doesn't seem to help.

From the sexual history of the couple it was learned that even in the very beginning of marriage the husband seemed to have an exceptionally low sexual drive. He "obliged" his wife more often early in marriage, but if she didn't approach him, he would go for weeks at a time without making any overtures. He just didn't seem to have very much interest in sex, and generally this condition existed from the very beginning.

Declining Interest. In other situations, the husband is very interested in sex during the honeymoon, and perhaps for a short time afterward, but then his interest declines.

Dr. David Mace tells the story of a husband who had a heart attack. When he was released from the hospital, he asked his cardiologist if he could resume sexual intercourse. The physician replied: "Yes, with your wife, by all means. But not with other women—I don't want you to get excited!" The physician's remark is quite indicative of what happens with many couples. The initial excitement wears off, so couples become less and less interested in intercourse as the years go on. One wife complained: "We had a fantastic sex life on our honeymoon, but it has been going downhill ever since." Even though sexual drive has started out at a high peak, the basic problem arises as the husband's drive declines.

But whether the drive has always been low, or whether it declines to a much lower level over the years, the basic question is why?

CONTRIBUTING FACTORS

Why do some men have a low sexual drive, or develop it, while other men have a sexual appetite that is sufficient? There are a number of widely contrasting views on the exact nature of the sexual drive, and especially on whether its intensity is determined mainly by physiological or psychological components, or by both.

Physiological and Biological Factors. The traditional assumption is that the sexual drive is physiological or biological in nature and that individual differences in sexual appetite are due to differences in biological endowments. Thus, in a 1945 text, *Psychology of Sex Relations,* Theodor Reik wrote:

The crude sex drive is a biological need which represents the instinct and is conditioned by chemical changes within the organism. The urge is dependent on inner secretions, and its aim is the relieving of physical tension. (Reik, 1945, p. 90)

This view emphasizes that sexual tension builds up as semen and sperm count multiply, and that the tension created demands release. Freud spoke of the need in males to discharge "sexual products," accompanied by physical pleasure. (Freud, 1953) It is assumed, therefore, that basic biological differences account for differences in the rapidity with which tension builds up and demands release, and that this accounts in part for the differences in drive.

It is recognized, also, that the degree of intensity of sexual drive is dependent partially upon the level of male hormones (androgens), and especially testosterone, in the bloodstream. This emphasis upon hormonal influences makes it quite evident that there are enormous physical differences in sexual endowment, capacity, and drive in different males. Consequently, the administration of testosterone may increase the general level of sexual interest and response in some men, especially in those persons who clearly indicate a hormonal deficiency. (See Chapter 12.)

A number of studies have measured the effects of castration on male sexual behavior. Ancient and primitive peoples have always linked physical maturation and the process of reproduction with the presence of male testes. If boys were castrated before puberty, they never developed typical male traits. They remained boyish in body build; their voices stayed at a high pitch; they never showed the usual sexual drive and interest in women.

The picture is completely different in adult males, however. If males are castrated after years of normal sexual activity, sexual drive may decline in some, but others show a complete retention of sexual function for years. This may be due to the fact that other parts of the body may partially compensate for the loss of testicular hormones, but it is due to the fact also that sexual drive is more than a biological component. It is strongly influenced by psychological or cultural forces.

Psychological Factors. Psychological conditioning varies from male to male while growing up. Some boys are raised to learn to inhibit their sexual drives and feelings. Reference has already been made to the inhibiting effect of a strict religious upbringing, or of a view of sex which makes it dirty or immoral. If this philosophy is drummed into a boy year after year, one would expect that his sexual interest would be inhibited as he grew older. Other boys are raised just the opposite: they are taught that sex is one of the most important aspects of life, that to repress sexual urges is unhealthy, that they ought to be expressed at each and every available opportunity. Ordinarily, those reared within this environment would be less inhibited and would manifest greater interest in sex and a stronger sexual drive as they reached maturity.

Cultural Factors. Furthermore, there are significant differences from culture to culture in the interest and frequency of sexual stimulation to which males are exposed. In our contemporary society, boys are repeatedly exposed to sexual stimuli on all sides, especially from advertising and the media. As a result, many boys grow up thinking and talking about sex constantly, and, when they mature, they desire to express sex at every opportunity. Anthropologists report on the compulsive interest in sex in our society in comparison with primitive cultures. They report that the urgency of sexual need in these primitive societies is in no way equal to the urgency of sexual need which is evident in our culture. As a result, any male in our culture who does not seem to have a compulsive and constant interest in sex is considered abnormal. He doesn't measure up to societal standards, even though he may be considered fairly average as far as some cultures are concerned. This is especially true in a society like ours that is also now emphasizing a high degree of sexual interest and drive in women. Males who are not meeting these intense sexual needs are considered to have a below normal sexual drive. Thus, the strength of the sexual drive is not only conditioned by the environment in which each male grows up, but its measurement is also relative to the standards determined by the culture.

Sexual Capacity, Performance, and Drive. It is helpful also to make a distinction between *sexual capacity, sexual performance,* and *sexual drive. Sexual capacity* is determined by the ability of the nervous, vascular, and muscular systems to respond to sexual stimuli and to recuperate from this experience to the point where orgasm can again be experienced. This capacity varies from male to male and represents the actual physical differences between individuals. Actually, the sexual activity of many men is considerably below their actual capacity.

Sexual performance, although limited in its upper extremes by capacity, varies according to physical and psychological factors, and also depends partially upon opportunity. Some males are low performers; they have a nervous system that is not too responsive to stimuli; they have a low level of male hormones to trigger sexual interest and drive; they have been conditioned to inhibit sexual instincts and responses as much as possible; they do not receive as much pleasure in sexual activity; and, perhaps, they may not even have as much opportunity for sexual expression. Consequently, their sexual performance is quite low.

Sexual drive is the strength or intensity with which the individual wishes sexual expression. Drive can have a physical base, but it seems to be very largely a psychologically conditioned component and may vary considerably from individual to individual and from time to time in the same

individual. More and more, psychological conditioning has
been emphasized as playing the most important role in influencing sexual motivation.

IMPROVING THE SITUATION

Discovery. We have emphasized repeatedly that the first
step in solving sexual problems is to discover the causes, and
that physical factors should be checked out first. A hormonal
evaluation can be made at any laboratory upon the recom-
mendation of a qualified physician. A blood sample is taken,
and the testosterone level determined by laboratory test.
Most physicians also want to get a complete medical and
sexual history to uncover any physical factors that are significant. Is the husband in good health? Does he have or has he
had any illnesses or medical problems that might affect his
sexual drive? Is he taking any medicine or drugs that might
act as inhibitors? Is the low drive of recent origin, or has this
always existed? A sudden lowering of drive is indicative of
the onset of significant physical or emotional factors.

In the absence of physical factors, the most likely base for
loss of erotic appetite is a disturbance in the emotional and
psychosocial life of the individual. Sexual functioning is a
sensitive barometer which responds to shifting emotions, to
the climate of the marital relationship, and to life in general.
Consequently, most counselors explore every avenue that
might affect sexual functioning. Is the husband quite worried
or anxious about something? Does he seem depressed,
moody, upset, tense, or withdrawn? Is his sexual dysfunction
a symptom of incipient mental disturbance or illness? Has he
become preoccupied with his career or with economic problems to the exclusion of his marriage? Is there considerable
conflict or disturbance in his marriage? What are his feelings
toward his wife, and what is the degree of sexual interest
which he expresses in her? When he has intercourse, what is
the degree of pleasure that he derives? What does he like
most, what does he dislike most about his marriage, his wife,

his sexual life? Are there important factors in his environmental situation that are affecting the expression of sex?

Increasing Motivation. It has been suggested that sexual drive depends not only on capacity but on motivation, and this in turn depends partially on the degree of pleasure that a couple experience in their sexual relationship. Too often, after ten or twenty years of marriage, sex becomes boring and uninteresting. The problem here is how to make marital sex more exciting. There are a number of ways.

The couple can introduce variety into their established positions, procedures, times, and places. If they are used to making love in the same missionary position (face-to-face, with the husband superior), let them experiment with other positions: lying down, sitting, kneeling, standing up, face-to-face, front-to-back, side-by-side, from the rear, legs up, down, apart, or together, etc. Variety can be the spice of one's sexual life.

The couple can also vary the procedures, the routine of their love play. Are they used to pleasuring in a certain way? Vary the order and methods employed. They can experiment with oral techiques, various types of manual manipulation, massages, or use of body lotions. The number of innovations that couples can add to their usual procedures is endless. The wife and the husband who are careful about cleanliness, who are willing to court and woo each other in the way they dress (what's wrong with wearing a sexy nightgown for the husband who seems bored?), or with candlelight suppers or soft music, are adding romance and excitement to their sexual life.

The couple can also vary the times and places. If they're used to making love in the bedroom, how about the living room couch, the bathroom floor? How about going out parking and petting in the car? How about a motel room? How about the forest floor (in season, of course)? If they only make love at night, how about having intercourse for lunch?

Above all, little remembrances, considerate expressions of

love and affection in their daily lives, do more to keep the fires of romance burning than do a dozen different coital positions. A loving card, a single rose, may be all that is needed. Of course, no couple can expect to keep the intense excitement of the early days of courtship, but they certainly can expect to feel a deep, wonderful kind of love and affection that is meaningful and satisfying. But this does take careful attention.

The Need for Cooperation. In recent years, increasing numbers of women are rebelling against the whole idea of a woman as a sexual object, to be admired for her shapely figure or large bust. As one wife remarked: "I don't see why I have to make myself sexy to interest my husband. What's wrong with me the way I am? I have the feeling that all he's interested in is to take me to bed." This question reflects the real anxiety of a woman in love that her husband doesn't really love her for herself, but perceives her only as a sexual object.

Several things need to be said in reply. One, no wife wants to feel used. If she has the feeling that her husband is interested in her only for the purposes of sex, the burden falls upon the husband to show his total concern and love, and not only just before making love. Second, every wife fears the loss of her youthfulness and beauty, and wants to feel that her husband loves her totally, not just because he likes a part of her anatomy. Here again, is he in love with the whole woman? Third, it is equally important for the husband *and* the wife to make themselves desirable. Every husband needs to remember that if he expects his wife to be as attractive as possible (and he would be less than human if didn't expect this), then he also has an obligation to make himself as desirable to her as possible. A double standard just doesn't work. Today's women want equality. Making one's sexual life more exciting requires the efforts of two people, and not one.

And last, exciting sex depends on an exciting marriage, on the total relationship. If the husband and the wife both care, and if both are concerned about making their marriage relationship more exciting, then, in the process, their sexual life usually improves also. After all, aren't they usually without dress when they make love? And isn't the feeling between them more important than their physical dimensions?

The Ambitious Husband. One of the principal deterrents to marital bliss and sexual fulfillment is the ambitious, hard-driving husband who feels that his only contribution to the family is his paycheck and who feels that his responsibility for maintaining his marriage ends when he says "I do." As a result, he neglects his marital responsibilities and his wife's emotional and sexual needs.

All marriage counselors are aware of the fact that in 3 out of 4 cases of disturbed marriage, it is the wife who first calls the counselor to get help. One reason is that many more wives are dissatisfied with their marriage than are husbands. Another reason is the traditional concepts of sexual roles: women are supposed to be more concerned about their home and family than are men; men are supposed to be more concerned about business and making money.

As the situation now stands, the traditional roles of wives are changing. Their roles are more and more in the community and in the world of business as well as in the home. They seek greater sexual equality and fulfillment. But present data indicate that the average husband has not changed very much either in his concept or in the actual performance of his role. He is willing for his wife to share in earning income, and he may even be slightly more willing to take over some of the parental or housekeeping chores, but he still places the major burden for maintenance of the marriage upon his wife. If anything goes wrong, "it's her fault." Women's magazines are full of articles on how to make marriage work, how to improve sex with one's husband, how to be a better home-maker. But men's magazines seldom emphasize how the husband can be more romantic, how he can be a better husband, what his responsibilities are in making his marriage work.

Part of the modern wife's frustration is not only sexual, it is total: How can I get my husband to be more interested in me, our marriage, our family? How can I get him to stay home more? How can I get him to be as interested in me as he is in his work? The burden of responsibility is with modern husbands: to learn to be better partners, not just better lovemakers.

PART IV

FEMALE
SEXUAL DYSFUNCTION

15

FEMALE FRIGIDITY

MANIFESTATIONS

Use of the Term. The word *frigidity* is frequently misused. It is often used in a derogatory sense as a label for women who don't respond sexually as the men think they should. Thus, one husband may accuse his wife of being frigid if she doesn't have sex every night, or even on one particular night. Another may label his wife frigid because she won't respond to him when he has alcohol on his breath. Another calls his wife frigid if she doesn't have an orgasm each and every time.

The word is unfair because it passes judgment, and that judgment may not be correct. One woman reported to her physician: "I guess I'm frigid." When the doctor asked why she thought she was frigid, she replied: "My husband thinks so." But the wife admitted that she had never had intercourse with any man except her husband. "Then how do you know whether you are frigid or not?" was the doctor's question. Actually, of course, the woman couldn't know for sure, since she had no basis for comparison. By what standard was the husband judging? And even if his wife was as cold as an iceberg, the real question is why? Was the husband doing something to which the wife objected? Was she cold and unresponsive because of him? Would she be the same if her husband were a different sort of man?

Degrees and Symptoms. For purposes of discussion here, *frigidity may be defined as a lack of desire for or a lack of pleasure in sexual relations.* But it manifests itself in so many different ways and to differing degrees. There is first of all the woman who seems totally uninterested in sex. These are women with a very low degree of sexual tension, who are just as happy if they never have intercourse, who may or may not ever experience orgasm. Reuben writes:

> For all practical purposes, the sexual organs don't exist. A woman afflicted with this condition has renounced all interest in sex and things sexual. She is misunderstood by her family and friends and relegated to social shadows as a "frustrated old maid," a title she certainly doesn't deserve. (Reuben, 1969, p. 126)

If such a woman does get married, she may react in several ways. She may be so unresponsive that she avoids intercourse whenever possible. She "freezes up" whenever her husband approaches her sexually. She may make things so unpleasant that he doesn't want to touch her. One such wife told her husband that he could sleep with a prostitute anytime he wanted as long as he left her alone! This wife also told her friends that she favored legalized prostitution so wives wouldn't be molested by their husband.

Other wives acquiesce to their husband's request for sex, but adopt the attitude that they want to "get it over and done with as soon as possible." These wives find intercourse a chore which they hate. Other wives consider it their "duty" to have intercourse with their husband and are proud of the fact that they "never deny him sex." But, for them, sex relations are worse than pulling teeth. They grin and bear it, but don't like it. It is doubtful whether over a period of time the husband likes it much either if the wife participates with clenched teeth. Of course, the woman who looks upon sex in marriage as her conjugal duty or obligation is also denying herself the opportunity of enjoying sex, and not giving herself a chance to respond.

Then there are wives who have some interest in intercourse, but only occasionally. They wouldn't be concerned at
all except they want to please their husband, and they are
worried because their husband is upset. These wives care,
but don't really know what to do about it. One wife confessed:

> I am twenty-eight years old, have three small children,
> and a good husband. My problem is I have no desire for
> intercourse. Maybe once or twice a month I may really
> want sex, but the rest of the time I try hard to avoid it. This
> attitude on my part really hurts my husband. I'd like to
> please him; I don't want him to think I don't love him. So
> I tell myself I'll do better, but I can't force myself. I'm so
> glad for some excuse to say no.

There are wives who responded at one time but who become less responsive as time goes on. One woman remarked:

> I am forty and although I never had a lot of interest in
> sex, I seem to have less as I get older. My husband is a
> wonderful person. He's kind and considerate, a good fa-
> ther, and a good provider. He has a lot of sex drive, and
> wants me to be more interested. My doctor tells me there's
> nothing wrong with me, but that doesn't help me much.
> I still think there's something I can do.

At the other extreme are the wives who appear very unresponsive on their honeymoon, or early in marriage, but who
become less inhibited with the passing of time. So-called
"honeymoon frigidity" is not at all uncommon. The new
bride may be young, uninformed, and inexperienced. She's
not sure what is going to happen, nor what she is supposed
to do. Her mother may have told her very little, or only
negative things, such as: "It hurts a lot the first few weeks, but
after a while you won't notice it so much." Or, "You probably
will bleed a lot, but most girls do." Or, "Now remember,
dear, it's a wife's duty to sleep with her husband, but try to
think about something else, and you won't mind so much."
Needless to say, such words of motherly advice do nothing to

improve the situation. Fortunately, many such wives overcome these negative teachings and go on to become very
responsive sexual beings. Many become multiorgasmic and
find they really enjoy sex and want it often.

Numerous wives are interested in sex, are quite willing to
have intercourse with their husband, but have little feeling
or pleasure in the experience. They do not become sexually
aroused, show very little sign of vasocongestion, lubrication,
or other indications of sexual excitement. They may also
show a total lack of feeling during intercourse itself. Because
of a lack of vaginal lubrication, intercourse may even be
painful. Something is happening to block response. Actually,
the completely unresponsive woman is very rare. Most respond in some situations but not in others, or with a particular person but not with others, or when stimulated in a particular way but not in other ways.

Then, finally, there are wives who become regularly
aroused to the plateau stage of response but who never or
rarely experience orgasm. This problem is discussed sepa-
rately in the next chapter.

Primary and Secondary Frigidity. A distinction should be
made between frigidity that has always existed *(primary frigidity)* and frigidity that has arisen out of recent happenings
(secondary frigidity). Complete and total primary frigidity is
actually quite rare. Most women who believe themselves to
be frigid discover with help that they are really not. After all,
most have all the necessary physical equipment to respond
sexually. They were created as sexual beings and the natural
thing is for them to respond. It is *not* true that a lack of
interest in sex or a lack of pleasure in it is normal female
behavior. It is abnormal. Something has gone wrong, physically or psychologically, and these causes can be discovered.

Husband's Reactions. Husbands react in different ways to
their wife's lack of interest or pleasure in sexual relations.
The husband who thinks it is his wife's duty to satisfy him and

proceeds with intercourse over his wife's objections is only compounding the problem. His wife grows to like sex even less. The same is true of the husband who seeks orgasm for himself but does not try to stimulate his wife to climax. How can she enjoy sex if she doesn't gain complete fulfillment?

There are husbands who persist, even though the wife objects in the beginning, but who make every effort to arouse the wife, to woo, court, and caress her to get her interested, and to make sex a pleasurable experience for her. They are able to help their wife overcome her resistance and to thoroughly enjoy the experience.

At the opposite extreme are the husbands who just withdraw. They are hurt; they are angry; they are mystified; but they just acquiesce. As far as their wife is concerned, they have learned to accept and live with her disinterest in sex. The problem with this reaction, however, is that very few husbands really have accepted the situation. They feel it is futile to argue with their wife, so they don't, but this does not mean they really accept the frustration emotionally. Some husbands use their wife's lack of responsiveness as an excuse for having extramarital relations. One husband remarked:

> My wife really doesn't like intercourse, so I go elsewhere. I feel that this is the best answer for me. I can't go without sex, and I would never think of divorce, so I have a girl friend on the side. I sleep with her several times a week.

Other husbands aren't unfaithful, but they take out their hurt and resentment in many different ways. It is their way of getting even. Of course, the problem here is that the husband-wife relationship becomes more and more strained, bitter, and conflicting. The husband who says and does mean things because he is sexually rejected is only compounding the problem. Many such marriages (sometimes soon, sometimes not until years later) end in a bitter divorce. If divorce never happens, the marriage becomes a source of much unhappiness. One such couple fight bitterly, constantly. Verbal and physical abuse is a daily occurrence. How they can live in such a fashion is a mystery. Their daughter is a neurotic wreck. They are very, very unhappy persons.

Many husbands react in unpredictable fashion to sexual frustration. One time they become violent, or at least angry. At other times, they withdraw or pout, or won't speak to their wife for days afterward. At other times, they become very sweet and overindulgent. One wife commented: "The only time my husband is nice to me is when he wants sex. As soon as he starts to help me with the dishes, and butter me up, I know what he has in mind."

Unfortunately, many times it does not do the husband any good. His wife usually finds excuses.

It is important for the couple to recognize that the problem is *their* problem—not just the wife's problem, not just the husband's problem, but their problem together. It affects them and their marriage. It is important for them both to be willing to get at the cause of the difficulty and seek remedial help. Most such problems can be solved—if the couple are willing.

No husband should have to live with continual sexual frustration. No wife should have to remain unresponsive and unable to enjoy sexual expression. If they really love each other, they will do everything possible to improve the situation. This may require outside help.

ORGANIC AND PHYSICAL CAUSES

Most of the causes of frigidity are psychological in origin, arising out of the past or present to create blocks to sexual response. However, since organic factors play a role, it is wise to probe for physical factors if these might be present. These factors have been outlined in Chapter 3 and other places. Physical causes include the following:

Drugs. The overuse of drugs, particularly those which have a sedative effect—alcohol, barbiturates, tranquilizers, narcotics—may lower sexual drive. Many other drugs also cause problems. The doctor should be consulted if any type of medication is taken that might influence sexual drive.

Hormonal Influences. Hormonal imbalances also play a role. It is well known that the male hormones, the androgens, play the decisive role in stimulating sexual drive in women as well as men. If for some reason *adrenalectomy* (removal of adrenals) or *hypophysectomy* (removal of the pituitary gland) is necessary, a marked drop in androgens occurs, together with a lessening of sexual interest. This interest is ordinarily restored when hormonal therapy is instituted to regulate the deficiencies.

Oophorectomy. What about the effect of *oophorectomy* (removal of the ovaries) on sexual drive? Dr. Robert Kolodny reports that only a small minority of women report a lessening of sexual interest and activity following the removal of the ovaries. (Kolodny, 1975, p. 122) It is true that the ovaries produce estrogen. With the ovaries gone, the production of the ovarian estrogen ceases and is only partially made up by the secretion of estrogen by the adrenals. But, as already suggested, estrogen is not *the* controlling factor in female sexual drive. Ordinarily, therefore, even though the supply of estrogen from the ovaries is cut off when the ovaries are removed, sexual interest remains.

Menopause. The same principle applies at *menopause*. In this case, the ovaries atrophy, die, cease to function. The supply of estrogen is cut off, but sexual interest remains. It even increases in some women because the fear of pregnancy is gone. If sexual drive declines, it is usually due to psychological reactions to menopause or to physical side effects of the menopause such as hot flashes, vaginitis, fatigue, chest pain, migraine headaches, insomnia, depression, irritability, etc. The estrogen may help, not because of increases in sexual drive, but because it minimizes these other menopausal symptoms, the woman feels better, and she is more interested in sex as a result. Dr. Robert Greenblatt says that "the administration of estrogens postmenopausally will restore the sexual drive in about 25 percent of women with secondary loss of libido." (Greenblatt, 1975, p. 122) He goes on to suggest that physicians meet with greater success if androgens are added to the estrogen regime, since androgens may restore the sexual drive in women who once enjoyed sexual expression. However, many physicians are hesitant to administer estrogen postmenopausally because of risks to older women. They also are very careful about giving androgens because of possible side effects such as acne, enlargement of the clitoris, deepening of the voice, sodium retention, edema, etc. For these reasons, any decisions about the use of hormones to increase sexual drive have to be made by the woman's own physician after all factors have been considered.

Just recently, the American Chemical Society has announced the experimental use of a new drug, bromocryptine, which restores the production of sperm in men and induces menstruation in women afflicted with cessation of the menstrual cycle. The drug also drastically sharpens sexual desire and has led to normal sexual activity in women who "have never had any erotic feelings in their lives." The drug is still in the experimental stages, however, and is not available to the general public. ("Notable Success Reported with Sex Drugs," *Portland Press Herald,* July 30, 1977) Whether the drug proves its usefulness with large populations of women, and without serious side effects, remains to be seen.

Birth Control Pill. There are sometimes effects on sexual behavior in women taking the birth control pill (which contains estrogen and progesterone). Most studies show that women on the pill have sexual intercourse more frequently (20 percent higher) than women using other methods of contraception. However, this is probably due to the removal of the fear of pregnancy and not to physical factors. It has been found that some women on the pill for a long period of time may show declining interest, probably because the high levels of estrogen counteract the influence of androgens on sexual drive. If this happens, physicians usually recommend another contraceptive method for a while at least.

Hysterectomy. What about the effects of *hysterectomy* (removal of the uterus) on sexual drive? From a physical point of view, it should have no effect. If, prior to the operation, the doctor explains to the woman exactly what is going to happen, and assures her that sexual capacity is not affected, she is more likely to show no change at all after the operation. Hysterectomy does *not* mean removing the ovaries, so the woman does not experience the symptoms of menopause (except for the cessation of her periods). Dr. Charles E. Flowers writes:

> A properly performed vaginal or abdominal hysterectomy should not interfere with normal sex relations. If she has had a satisfactory sex relationship prior to hysterectomy, she will continue to have one after it. However, if there were problems and difficulties preceding the hysterectomy, it is rare that the operation improves the sex relationship unless there was a fear of pregnancy. (Flowers, 1975, p. 184)

Of course some women do become sexually less responsive following a hysterectomy, but this is due to psychogenic factors and is not inherent in physical results of the operation.

Mastectomy. The surgical removal of the breast *(mastectomy)* also need not affect a woman's sexual life, unless she has negative psychological reactions from the operation, or unless her husband is affected adversely. It is true that many men have made breast beauty an important aspect of sexual attractiveness. But not all men have this attitude. Thousands of husbands enjoy sex with their wives after a mastectomy.

There are some women who are so ashamed of their looks after the operation that they rule out any opportunity for sexual intercourse because of what they assume their husband's reactions will be. But the majority of husbands are so glad their wife has been restored to health that they really don't care. With the right attitudes, couples can still enjoy sex as much as before.

Sterilization. What are the effects of *tubal ligation* (female sterilization) on sexual drive? There isn't any from a physical point of view. Tubal ligation involves cutting and tying the Fallopian tubes so egg cells cannot pass into the uterus and sperm cells cannot enter the tubes and reach an ovum. Sterilization does not involve ovarian removal unless an ovary is diseased. Neither does it involve the removal of the uterus (even though a hysterectomy, of course, does render it impossible for a woman to conceive). Most women have increased sexual interest and enjoyment after sterilization because the fear of pregnancy has been removed. If the woman is quite relieved of any dread of pregnancy, she usually becomes much more responsive. If she does react negatively, because of religious feelings or for other reasons, or because she did not want to be sterilized but had to be for health reasons, she may show diminished sexual interest and enjoyment, but the cause is psychological, not physical. It is due to her negative emotional reactions to what has happened. She may need counseling to work through her negative emotions.

Physical Illnesses. Any type of debilitating physical illness will affect sexual drive and response. The wife who is anemic, tired, and rundown, who has severe protein, mineral, or vitamin deficiencies, may not feel like having sexual intercourse because she doesn't feel well. Even minor illnesses—a bad cold, the flu, a headache—affect sexual response. Fatigue, exhaustion, stress, and overwork are major deterrents to sexual enjoyment. Numerous major illnesses also interfere with one's sexual life, as do local diseases such as urinary tract or vaginal infections. Any problem that makes intercourse painful should also be investigated. (See Chapter 17.) It is important that the woman get good medical care if health problems are suspected.

PSYCHOLOGICAL CAUSES

The major causes of female frigidity are psychological, either originating in earlier experiences or relating to the woman's present relationships with her husband.

Early Conditioning. Any kind of intense, emotional experiences that negatively condition women against sex may influence their ability to respond later on. Emotional deprivation in childhood makes it harder for adult women to be warm and affectionate. The father who hugs and kisses his infant daughter and says to her, "I love you," is helping her to express love and affection through physical means. Most children need a lot of cuddling and physical assurance of love as they are growing up.

One mother came to me because she was worried that her eight-year-old daughter wanted to sit on the lap of every man who came into the house. "If she's like this now, what's she going to be like when she's mature? Is she going to throw herself at every man she meets?" was the mother's anxious question. It was obvious that the girl was starved for affection and that her lap sitting was her way of fulfilling her own emotional needs. I asked: "Do you hug and kiss your daughter yourself? And is your husband demonstrative toward her?"

"No, we aren't gushy in that way, but she knows that we love her," was the mother's reply.

In the conversation that followed, I explained to the mother the reasons for her daughter's behavior and suggested that she and her husband both use every opportunity to express their love of her through hugging, kissing, and cuddling. "Give her so much love and affection that she has no need to seek it with other persons," was my suggestion.

What happens when a girl does not receive affection? Either one of two things. She may react as did the girl in the previous example and become exceptionally demanding, so that when she is married she will seek constant reassurance and repeated demonstration of affection from her husband, or she may withdraw from close associations with people, become cold and unresponsive whenever anyone tries to get close to her, as her defense against rejection. In this case, her behavior is a reflection of the coldness and isolation she experienced as a child. *One of the best assurances of the ability to respond sexually is to have been brought up by parents who are warm and affectionate toward their children.* Adults learn to express love by having been loved.

A puritanical upbringing may be responsible for inhibiting the wife's ability to respond sexually. Unfortunately, in the past, women did not have permission to be sexual beings. Their sexuality was denied and repressed because it was considered improper for a woman. Even today, some physicians or clergymen tell the woman who is sexually unresponsive: "Don't worry about it, a lot of women are that way." The implication is that this is normal behavior for a woman. As a result of this attitude, many girls today grow up denying their sexual feelings in order to conform to society's image of "proper" behavior for girls. This makes it most difficult for them to respond sexually in marriage. If everything a child has been taught about sex is negative, how is she going to feel right about being sexy? Such a repressive attitude becomes an effective barrier to female responsiveness.

Early Traumatic Experiences. One of the questions frequently asked is what is the effect of childhood molestation, incest, or rape on later adult sexuality? The effect will depend largely upon how upsetting the experience was for the child. The more she was upset, the more likely she will be affected afterward. If the experience was a brief episode, involving older children or an adult, and was not painful, and the parents didn't get too disturbed in their child's presence, the girl may not think too much about it, so the episode will have no permanent negative effects. Most children do a certain amount of "peeking" and "playing" while growing up. Statistics also indicate that about 25 percent of women have had some sexual experience such as being fondled by a man or seeing an exhibitionist during childhood. Most such experiences do not have an overwhelming effect on development in the young girl. But if the incident involves much actual molestation or even child rape, and particularly if the incident is repeated over a period of time, the child may be very upset. If the adult threatens bodily harm if the girl tells, or if the encounter causes physical pain or discomfort, so that the girl is quite frightened, the emotional scars of such negative conditioning may last a long time.

One physician in Philadelphia treated 13 women who were victims of childhood rape. Eleven were raped by persons they knew, 6 of these by their own father. They were persons whom these young girls trusted and even loved. The girl's age, her relationship to the offender, the physical and emotional circumstances surrounding the rape (brutality, weapons, threats, forced perversions, etc.), the quality and consistency of the mother's response, police reactions, and the length of time intervening between the incident and psychotherapy, were all influential in influencing the girl's postrape emotional recovery. (Peters, 1975, p. 300)

Negative Reactions to Events in Adulthood. Secondary frigidity may develop out of events that prove upsetting. One example is that of a twenty-three-year-old girl who terminated an unwanted pregnancy with an abortion. The woman did not seem to develop postpartum blues or post-abortive depression, but she would not permit her husband to have intercourse with her, insisting it was "too soon." Actually, four months had elapsed since pregnancy was interrupted; the doctor had assured her that everything was back to normal, but she refused to listen to medical assurance. In other respects she was an affectionate and efficient housewife, was willing to indulge in sexual play with her husband to satisfy his needs, but still refused intercourse. Her deep-seated fear of pregnancy prevented her from having intercourse.

Many times a wife's frigidity develops out of something her husband says or does. One tragic case was that of a young bride of twenty who had been married only a week when she returned to her minister, who had officiated at her wedding.

> I was looking forward to my honeymoon so much. The wedding was beautiful. John and I went to this lovely hotel by the ocean. But the first time we made love he started to tell me about all his old girl friends that he had slept with. I tried to tell him that I wasn't interested, but he kept on—even going into detail about how each one made love. I was completely shocked. For one thing, I didn't even know he had intercourse with anybody before me. For another thing, why would he want to talk about it—and on our wedding night? Doesn't he have any regard for me? How did he think I would feel? I tell you how I felt: I was hurt and angry, so much so that I got up out of that bed, dressed, and moved out.

The woman did go for repeated counseling sessions with her minister, but was not able to change her feelings. Counseling with the husband also, and with the two of them together, brought no real change of attitude on the part of the wife. She could not bear to think of sleeping with her husband again. She was divorced six months later.

Some wives react in a similar fashion when they discover that their husband has been unfaithful. As one wife remarked:

> I can never feel the same toward him again. After I first found out that he was sleeping with another woman, he was sorry, begged me to forgive him and give him another chance. So I did. But then just recently I found out he had

been sleeping with someone else. I can't ever trust him. And I just can't bear to let him near me. All I can think about is that he was doing the same thing with someone else.

In other cases, wives "freeze up" when the husband suggests some type of sexual activity which the wives find objectionable. In such cases, the wife is not really unresponsive at all; she only becomes so when requested to participate in a type of sexual activity she can't accept.

Emotional Illness and Depression. A wife who is ordinarily interested in intercourse but who becomes cold and indifferent may be experiencing emotional problems that are affecting her sexual life. It is important to find out the reasons. Is she particularly agitated, disturbed, or upset? Is she moody or depressed? One study of 27 women, ages twenty-five to sixty, who were admitted to outpatient treatment for severe mental depression showed the following symptoms (in contrast to women who were mentally healthy) (Bullock, 1972):

They rarely communicated with their spouse, seldom discussing problems together.

They showed a lower level of sexual intercourse, a greater disinterest in sex, and more problems in intercourse. Those who weren't interested in intercourse but who participated at the request of their husband were frequently without orgasm, or often reported dyspareunia.

The depressed women felt less affection for their spouse, and often felt resentment and guilt because of a sense of failure in the marital relationship.

The depressed women experienced more friction and had more arguments with their spouse. As hostility increased, nagging and explosive scenes were common.

The important thing about these women was the fact that the majority had mutually supportive marriages, including satisfying sexual relationships, prior to the depressive illness. Sexual problems developed as a result of the depression.

Disturbed Marital Relationships. Disturbance in the marital relationship is deeply disturbing to many women. Some can continue an active and at least a physically satisfying sexual relationship with their husband even in the face of severe marital problems. Most wives cannot. Ard writes:

> Humans interact sexually usually within the context of a relationship and the quality of the relationship can affect the sexual responses. . . . If some women feel that love is no longer in the relationship, they will become frigid or at least evidence "colder" sexual responses than formerly. (Ard, 1974, p. 85)

How the wife feels toward her husband is especially important in its influence on her sexual response. His appearance, his masculinity, his intelligence, his character traits, his drive, his manners—any number of things have to appeal to her before she can respond to him sexually. If in her eyes he is a social misfit, a financial failure, a slob, a perfectionist, or other negative images, the marriage is in trouble and sexual relations may be difficult. How can she go to bed with someone she dislikes or does not respect?

This is especially likely to happen when a woman marries too young or too hastily, before she is knowledgeable about men and really knows the type of man she most likes. Or it happens if a woman marries on the rebound. Jilted by one lover whom she believes she is madly in love with, she marries another man out of hurt and a desire to get even. She may discover she really didn't know him, or even like him in the first place.

Love and sex may both be affected by marked changes in the marital situation. Belliveau and Richter tell of a couple who had been married twenty-three years when they were referred for treatment. The wife had been orgasmic and multiorgasmic for twelve years of marriage. In the twelfth year, the husband was fired from his job, was unable to find employment for eighteen months, became depressed, and started to drink. The frequency and quality of the couple's sexual activity began to decline. When the wife found out that her husband was having an affair with another woman, arguments began, and the wife moved to a separate bedroom. (Belliveau and Richter, 1970, p. 129)

TREATMENT

Diagnosis. The type of treatment needed to help with the difficulty will depend upon the sources of the problem. Is there an organic problem or illness which has resulted in sexual dysfunction? Is the woman taking any drugs that may affect her sexual drive and pleasure? Is the problem due to a basic hormonal imbalance? Is the cause in the distant past in the way the wife was brought up? Did she become negatively conditioned against sex because of parental teachings or traumatic experiences? Has she experienced any trauma in her adult years that has affected her sexual responsiveness? Is she going through an emotional upset that has affected her sexual activity? What about the relationship with her husband? How does she feel toward him? Has he done anything in the past, or is he doing anything now, that prevents her from responding to him? Is the marriage relationship disturbed or harmonious? A serious consideration of these questions may help to determine the next step. A competent sex therapist will want to get answers to these questions, and to others like them, before an intelligent evaluation can be made.

Medical Checkup. As suggested, a medical checkup is advisable to rule out any physical difficulties, or to discover any that may be present. Such an examination ought to keep in mind any problems that would have an effect on the woman's sexual life.

Symptom-focused Sex Therapy. Symptom-focused sex therapy as presently practiced doesn't overlook organic problems, negative childhood conditioning, traumatic experiences, mental health, or disturbed marriage as causes of frigidity. Most sex therapists suggest a complete medical work-up, take sexual and marital histories, and utilize counseling and psychotherapy as needed, but they assign sexual tasks, as already discussed in Chapter 5 and elsewhere, as a means of counteracting negative conditioning, traumatic events, or disturbed marital relationships. By concentrating on the woman's feelings, and on her responses as various pleasuring and lovemaking techniques are employed, in nondemand situations, the woman begins to be able to relax and enjoy the caressing and to slowly respond to her husband's love play. For the first time, she may feel that sex is pleasurable. She is urged to "be selfish," to let herself enjoy it, not to worry about how her husband is feeling, or whether or not she will have an orgasm. Some wives never allow themselves to be stimulated long enough to respond. They become nervous, anxious, or worry about whether or not they are pleasing their husband, so they urge him to go ahead and have his orgasm, never giving themselves a chance to become aroused ahead of time. This is why the wife is urged, for now, to concentrate on her feeling rather than on her husband's.

But in nondemand pleasuring, orgasm does not enter in, at least initially. The couple proceed from nongenital stimulation, to genital stimulation without orgasm, to orgasm, to nondemand coitus, and finally to full coitus with orgasm. Procedure may vary from therapist to therapist, but the principles are similar even though the time schedules and tasks that are assigned differ.

In the meantime, the husband's attention is focused on how best to excite his wife. For the first time, he may be learning how to please her. The couple are urged to communicate, she to tell him what she likes and what she doesn't like, and he to check with her to find out what she most desires. Over a period of time, light, teasing, gentle play, where the husband gently touches her body, her nipples, her labia, her clitoral area, the vaginal entrance, become doubly erotic and exciting. When intercourse is begun, most therapists suggest the female superior position, so the wife can move in ways most conducive to her sexual pleasure.

Kaplan outlines three advantages to this pleasure-oriented sexual approach. First, the wife is relieved of the pressure of having to produce a response, so her anxiety and defenses are not aroused and her enjoyment is not curtailed. Second, the exercises are planned to evoke sexual excitement, to provide her with erotic pleasure, and, third, inevitably the husband and the wife become more sensitive to each other's sexual needs and reactions. When the wife begins to realize that her husband enjoys making her happy, and when she begins to have sexual pleasure, she no longer tries to avoid stimulation. (Kaplan, 1974, p. 368)

16

ORGASM DYSFUNCTION

WOMEN AND ORGASM

How Women Feel. There is no question about the desirability of orgasm. Women report:

> Orgasm feels great! Like a combination of intense pleasurable sensations plus an ecstatic frenzy of love, energy and emotion, all mixed together.
>
> Orgasms are a renewal of all my senses, an awakening of life, spring, refreshing, sparkling, exciting, and a complete relief of everyday boredom.
>
> Orgasm. The most fantastic sensation I've ever experienced. (Hite, 1976, p. 129)

In the past, there was a tendency to minimize the necessity and importance of orgasm for women. Because many women didn't have an orgasm, some persons felt this was a natural state of affairs, that the situation could be accepted as quite normal. In recent years, however, this point of view has been proven quite fallacious. Women not only can have an orgasm but they can have multiple orgasms, and have a far greater capacity for orgasm than do men. (See Chapter 4.) Modern feminists have come to resent deeply the myth that women do not need orgasm, which they feel has been perpetuated by men. One woman remarked:

> Whoever said orgasm wasn't important for a woman was undoubtedly a man. Good sex expresses love, relaxation, and letting go plus pure body pleasure. (Hite, 1976, p. 129)

Other women deeply resent the idea that it is important for a woman to have orgasm only for the sake of her husband. If she doesn't, she's afraid he will feel he has failed, that he is not manly, that his ego will be shattered. As one wife commented:

> I "perform" and boost his ego and confidence and love for me with an orgasm. I do not *like* to think of myself as a performer, but I feel judged, and also judge myself, when I don't have an orgasm. (Hite, 1976, p. 130)

Today's woman feels the social pressure on her as a woman to experience orgasm. Once it was discovered that females had such an enormous capacity for orgasm, individuals began to feel less than womanly if they did not.

> I can enjoy sex without orgasm, but psychologically I feel like I'm a failure, like a not totally functioning woman. (Hite, 1976, p. 131)

Other women express their sense of frustration and anger over the fact that their husband has an orgasm and they don't.

> I feel confused and cheated when I don't have an orgasm, and I lie there watching him having his. (Hite, 1976, p. 135)
>
> If my husband comes before I have a chance, I am left shaky and sick to my stomach and resentful and angry. (Hite, 1976, p. 147)

Effect on Marriage. In the long run, lack of orgasm not only robs the individual woman of a great deal of pleasure and satisfaction, but sex becomes so frustrating for her that she may grow to dislike it intensely. Ultimately, this will affect her relationship with her husband and her marriage.

> I've tried everything, but I've never had one. I feel that having an orgasm would leave me more satisfied and satiated. . . . I feel very frustrated and insecure without them. It causes me more unhappiness than anything else in my

life. I'm not sure that I want to stay married to my husband
because of such an unfulfilled sex life. (Hite, p. 1976, p. 206)

Over a period of time, the woman's inability to achieve orgasm, and her anticipation of failure when she makes love,
may cause secondary frigidity. As one woman remarked:
"Why should I be interested in sex when I don't get anything
out of it? How would a man like it if he never had an orgasm?" It is important to the woman herself and to her marriage that her lovemaking culminate in orgasm.

PATTERNS AND PREVALENCE

Percentages. What percentage of women do not have orgasm? According to Kaplan, only about 8 to 10 percent of the
sexually active female population have never experienced an
orgasm, with about 90 percent of all women able to achieve
orgasm by some means. (Kaplan, 1974, p. 340) These figures
are in close agreement with those of the Hite report in which
12 percent of women reported they had never had orgasm.
(Hite, 1976, p. 230)

This does not mean, however, that orgastic women always
achieve orgasm through intercourse. In the Hite report, only
about 30 percent of those who had orgasm did so regularly
from intercourse, another 22 percent had orgasm rarely
from intercourse, and an additional 19 percent could have an
orgasm during intercourse provided the clitoris was stimulated by hand at the same time. Twenty-nine percent of
women who had orgasm reported that they did not during
intercourse itself. (Hite, 1976, p. 231) This means that the
only way they could have orgasm was through manual stimulation of some kind.

Dr. Seymour Fisher conducted a five-year study of 300
relatively young, married women of middle-economic standing and found that only about 39 percent reported that they
had orgasm always or nearly always during intercourse, but
this also included those who used clitoral stimulation by hand

during intercourse. Only 20 percent of the women never acquired a push to orgasm from manual stimulation. (Fisher, 1973)

These findings are especially significant since in the past it was assumed that the most "mature" and "normal" way to have orgasm was through vaginal stimulation through penile thrusting. This idea was first expounded by Freud. He taught that women first start out having orgasms through masturbation, which involves the stimulation of the clitoris, but to be "mature," women have to learn to achieve orgasm through sexual intercourse, and specifically through vaginal stimulation by the penis. Women who do not achieve orgasm this way remain "fixated" and are not "fully developed." It was largely through Freud's teachings that a distinction was developed between a "clitoral orgasm" and a "vaginal orgasm."

This myth was exploded by Masters and Johnson. They showed that, physically speaking, there is only one type of orgasm, that an orgasm is an orgasm is an orgasm, no matter how achieved. (Masters and Johnson, 1966) As a matter of fact, it is far easier for most women to achieve orgasm through clitoral stimulation than by vaginal penetration, and, furthermore, greater physical excitement is developed through manual manipulation. Women report that clitoral orgasms are "sharper," "stronger," "higher," "more definite," but also "more localized" and "lonelier." Orgasms with vaginal penetration are "softer," "more diffuse," "more tender," "less sharp," more often involve the "whole body," and are described by some wives as "longer," with a "slower decline in feeling." (Hite, 1976, p. 187)

In spite of the greater intensity of orgasm with clitoral stimulation, the great majority of women like and want vaginal penetration. It is described by some women as more satisfying physically and psychologically. They like the warmth, the closeness, the feeling of being hugged and of being united with another human being. Intercourse is a means of being accepted, and of communication. It is a way of getting closer physically and emotionally than through others means. Women report:

> During intercourse, I feel secure and wanted, whole, warm, loved, womanly.
> During intercourse I feel secure, assured of his love, and protected. It feels good to my mind, body, and heart. (Hite, 1976, p. 424)

Intercourse becomes an affirmation of caring, and the integration of two people in love.

But herein lies the dilemma. The majority of women can have orgasms more easily and more intensely through masturbation. Some can have orgasms only in this way. But the majority also prefer intercourse, since they feel that it is a more satisfying experience. However, a significant minority of women can't have orgasm through intercourse alone. This dilemma led one woman to remark that she wished her clitoris were inside her vagina so she could have an orgasm through intercourse alone.

The dilemma remains a dilemma only if couples take the attitude that "no hands" intercourse is the only way to go. There are some wives who feel this way, and there are some husbands who say they ought to be able to make their wife come herself without any help. Some husbands even go so far as to say that they strongly dislike touching their wife manually, that it is "perverted." They are even more opposed to their wife stimulating herself during intercourse. But the results of such attitudes can be disastrous. Some wives simply can't have an orgasm without manual manipulation of the clitoral area, before and during intercourse, and because they can't enjoy intercourse as a result, become frigid if they don't achieve a climax. One wife commented.

> My husband made me feel that it was disgusting to touch myself. He let me know he didn't enjoying touching me with his hand either. After that, I felt ashamed to touch him. Now, I'm completely cold with him.

It is time that the record be set straight. There is nothing perverted, unnatural, or harmful (physically or mentally) about manual stimulation of the clitoral area before or during intercourse, whether that stimulation is accomplished with the penis, the hands, the tongue, or a vibrator. If the wife can't have her orgasm with her husband's penis inside her, but can if he withdraws and caresses her clitoris with his hand or tongue, then let him do that. He can excite his wife through foreplay, have his own orgasm through coitus, withdraw, and stimulate her manually. Or he can stimulate her to the point of orgasm before entering, then enter quickly while she has her orgasm, and then thrust to orgasm himself. If he lies close to her during manual stimulation, the experience can be as meaningful and enjoyable as orgasm through intercourse. If the wife can have an orgasm only during intercourse when she is in the female superior position, and while he is also manually caressing the clitoris, then let him do it that way. A few wives can only have a climax through cunnilingus. Then so be it. The important thing is that the couple totally participate, with full expression of love and feeling for each other, and that they both are satisfied.

Not all experts agree with this viewpoint. Part of the disagreement is over the explanation of the way the clitoris is stimulated during intercourse. Masters and Johnson, Sherfey (Sherfey, 1973), and others emphasize two mechanisms by which the clitoris is stimulated during intercourse: traction on the clitoral hood and pressure on the pubic area. During coitus, the thrust of the penis exerts tension on the folds of the labia minora, which is transmitted to the clitoral hood. As the hood moves up and down, it provides tactile stimulation to the shaft and glans of the clitoris. The right kind of rhythmic pressure applied to the mons pubis during masturbation accomplishes the same thing. As Sherfey puts it:

> Mons area friction will have exactly the same effect on the prepuce-glans action as the penile thrusting motion:

the prepuce is rhythmically pulled back and forth over the glans. (Sherfey, 1973, p. 111)

The only problem with this explanation is that it doesn't work for all women. One physician compared it to pulling the skin of the man's scrotum back and forth so the skin around the upper tip of the glans would move and stimulate the penis. It can be done, but it would take longer and require a great deal more foreplay for the man to have an orgasm. (The man would have to be patient and understand that it would not lead to an orgasm every time!) (Hite, 1976, p. 275) Hite sarcastically compared this with trying to stimulate the cheek of the face by pulling on one ear.

All authorities agree that penile thrusting within the vaginal canal is not the way many women have orgasms. They do agree that the most efficient method of becoming sexually aroused is direct stimulation of the clitoris or clitoral area itself. But, apparently, this does not always happen through coitus. In some women, the clitoris is well hidden beneath the folds of the skin of the hood, with the tip of the glans never showing. In many of these women, the clitoris is quite small. In others, the clitoris protrudes from the hood, so the glans itself can be caressed. In some females, there is a considerable distance between the vaginal orifice and the clitoris, making stimulation via penile thrusting difficult. Furthermore, the amount of stimulation needed to trigger female orgasm varies tremendously from woman to woman, and in the same woman under different circumstances. Some women can have a climax easily in any sexual situation; others require intense and lengthy clitoral stimulation. Some can fantasize eroticism and achieve orgasm without any physical contact. Others can have an orgasm through breast manipulation only. One physician told me she has some women who have an orgasm while having a vaginal examination. Other women have an orgasm while nursing their baby. One wife said she had an orgasm while only sitting next to a man. He never even touched her. Some women can rub their pubic area up against the arm of a chair or a folded towel and achieve climax. Another woman said she required three or four hours of direct clitoral stimulation before she could have an orgasm. Some women achieve orgasm only if their husband masturbates them; others can have an orgasm only while masturbating alone.

As far as intercourse itself goes, some women can have orgasms in any coital position, some after only a few coital thrusts. Others can have an orgasm in the male superior position, but only after considerable foreplay and thrusting. Others prefer the female superior position, which allows a great deal of clitoral pressure and stimulation. Some of these women require direct clitoral stimulation during coitus.

The point is, because of these great variations in orgasm response, one cannot agree with Freud that only the woman who has orgasm during intercourse is normal, and that the women who can have an orgasm only through direct coital stimulation lack "maturity." At the other extreme, one cannot agree with the extreme feminists who insist that clitoral stimulation alone is the norm, and that women who prefer intercourse with a man are subjecting themselves to "sexual slavery." If one were to posit a "norm," it would be somewhere in between these extreme views. But establishing a norm is not necessary. The important thing is for the wife to find orgastic release in relations with her husband through whatever techniques are most satisfying to her and acceptable to them both. However, since the majority of husbands and wives both prefer orgasm in association with coitus, the rest of the chapter will offer additional suggestions as to how this can be accomplished.

AROUSAL AND ORGASM

Adequate Time. One of the most frequent complaints of women is that the husband is in too much of a hurry, that he doesn't take enough time to arouse them before putting in his penis and thrusting to orgasm. Foreplay, if any, is too little, too short, too perfunctory, or unimaginative. The same routine is used over and over: a kiss, a few caresses of the breast, a few strokes of the pubis, and the husband is on top, banging away as fast and hard as possible to come as quickly as he can. As a result, the wife is barely aroused before the husband is finished. When he's through, he rolls over and goes to sleep, leaving the wife annoyed and frustrated.

Sufficient Stimulation. One way for the wife to be more likely to achieve orgasm during coitus itself is for the husband to be certain that she is aroused almost to the point of orgasm before intromission. If she has difficulty achieving climax through penile thrusting, then the husband can stimulate her through love play to the very edge of orgasm before insertion. If her excitement dies down before orgasm, he should withdraw, stimulate again, and reinsert. In some cases, it may be necessary to stimulate to the point where orgasm has already started at the time of intromission. Gradually, the time between love play and orgasm through penile thrusting can be extended.

As mentioned, in many cases the husband may have to stimulate the clitoris with his hand during intercourse, or his wife may prefer to stimulate herself. Either way, what is best for her is fine. If the wife is too embarrassed to stimulate herself, then by all means the husband should, but this is difficult in the husband superior position. In such cases, the wife superior position, the side-by-side position, or the wife on her stomach or side and the husband with his stomach next to her back may be preferred.

Communication. Some husbands are either woefully uninformed of their wife's needs, or, if informed, they are very selfish. Too many ignore their wife's need of orgasm and give insufficient attention to clitoral stimulation and arousal. Under such circumstances, it is important for the wife to be able to talk to her husband to give him oral instructions as to what she likes or does not like, or what feels good and how to achieve it. As one wife said: "He's always in the wrong place; he moves at the wrong moment, goes too fast, or presses too hard." If in these circumstances the wife can't tell her husband because she's too embarrassed, or because she feels he will get mad, or feel inadequate, the situation will not improve.

Neither is it possible to give complete instructions here that will suit all wives. Some wives don't like to have the clitoris itself touched, especially in the beginning of love play. These wives prefer that the massaging take place on either side or at the base, or by applying pressure to the mons. Some wives like vibrating the clitoris with a shaky movement of the hand on the mons. Others prefer a very delicate, light, teasing touch on the labia and on the clitoris itself. Some husbands rub so hard they hurt, or irritate. One wife complained: "He seems like he is trying to *erase* my clitoris." (Hite, 1976, p. 345) The only sure way for the husband to learn is for his wife to tell him.

Unfortunately, some wives try to tell the husband, but he won't listen. "I've tried to explain to my husband how important it is for him to play with my breasts first, but it seems like the next time, he's forgotten all about it." Men who are quite insecure believe they should be the experts, the aggressors, and that the wife should remain completely passive. If the wife makes any suggestions, the husband is insulted, believing he has failed. Such feelings reflect the old idea that the man must always be the aggressor. If both develop the philosophy of equal privileges and responsibilities in the lovemaking process, it is easier for the husband to be receptive to his wife's suggestions, and to want to please her. He needs to ask: "What do you like the most? How can I best please and pleasure you?" She needs to tell him, and he needs to listen and to respond.

Female Initiative. Most wives find that they become aroused more easily if they are quite active in helping to arouse themselves. There is no need for the wife to lie quietly hoping and waiting for her husband to stimulate her. For one thing, if she moves herself, it helps her to become aroused. One wife remarked: "If I move and grind and thrust, I find I become much more excited myself." Other wives emphasize that they have to learn to strain the muscles of their thighs, rectum, and vagina, that without tensing their body in a certain way they cannot achieve a climax. Some have to contract their vaginal muscles; some have to stretch with their legs together; others prefer their legs apart, with their pelvis thrust upward forcibly. As one woman said: "It took me a long time to learn to tense my body so that I could push myself over the brink." Hartman and Fithian write:

> She can maximize her turn-on not only by being an active participant, but by freely moving in nonthreatening ways to physical positions where movement is possible which will provide the maximum degree of sexual arousal. Sometimes rubbing her labia, for example, against her partner's thigh, either in the side by side or in the female superior position, will heighten arousal. (Hartman and Fithian, 1972, p. 187)

For another thing, most wives find that when they take an active role in caressing and stimulating their husband, they themselves become quite excited. Many wives find that seeing, touching, and fondling their husband's penis is highly stimulating to themselves.

Concentration. Most wives also agree that sexual arousal requires concentration. They have to think about themselves, and not just about what their husband is thinking and doing. They have to be free of distractions and lose themselves in the total experience. Most therapists advise wives to think erotic thoughts, to try to focus on highly stimulating sexual urges. The wife who starts thinking about what she is going to cook for supper is really not giving herself a chance. It doesn't matter what the image is: a mental picture of her husband's penis, a romantic scene from a movie, a couple making love, whatever the woman finds most exciting will help to stimulate her to orgasm. The important thing is for her to concentrate on the experiences at hand and to allow herself to be caught up in the rapture of her own passion.

POSITION AND ORGASM

Vaginal Sensitivity. Women vary greatly in their preferences of coital position. One reason is that women differ in where the vagina is sexually sensitive. We have already mentioned that vaginal stimulation through penile thrusting is not stimulating at all for some women. These have almost total vaginal anesthesia. All their erotic feelings are localized around the clitoris and the labia. Such women prefer positions that give them the maximum pressure on these organs. This "right" position for them may be the female superior position. Other women have areas of the vagina that are painful to touch. This may be due to tears or lesions in the vaginal wall which developed during childbirth. These women naturally seek coital positions that keep the penis from touching these painful areas. Some of these women prefer their legs spread far apart, with the penis entering from a certain angle. Other women have a loose, almost gapping vagina as a result of improper repairs or stitching after childbirth. These women may seek positions and angles that allow the penis to rub the external areas as much as possible. This may be either the female superior position or the male superior position, but with the wife's legs tightly together.

Clitoral Stimulation. Another reason for variations in preference of coital position is the need of some women for manual stimulation of the clitoris during intercourse. One wife likes to be on her stomach, with her buttocks slightly raised, her husband on top. In this position he can fondle her breasts and her clitoris during coitus. This brings the wife to orgasm easily.

Personal Preferences. Personal preferences, habit, and emotional factors also enter in. One wife remarked:

> I enjoy any position except my husband in a chair with me straddled on top. It seems too impersonal. He's too far away.

Some wives object to being on their hands and knees with their husband entering from the rear. "I feel like a dog" is a common reply. But the important thing is that a position be selected which will provide maximum stimulation. Some wives need to squat over their husband's penis so they can grind the mons and clitoris against the penile shaft; others prefer lying down on their husband, stomach to stomach, so they can thrust or oscillate in a certain way. Some prefer deep penetration, barely moving, allowing pressure on the mons to bring them to orgasm. Others prefer shallow penetration, with much movement in and around the vaginal orifice. Most important, the husband needs to be willing to find out from his wife what feels the best for her and what positions to use that can bring her to orgasm. Many husbands use first the position that assures that their wife will have an orgasm, then they switch to the position that he prefers.

PSYCHOLOGICAL FACTORS

As mentioned, there are some wives who cannot reach a climax at all through intercourse itself. Some of these wives simply do not find intercourse stimulating enough, but this can often be remedied by following suggestions already given. Other wives are just not able to let themselves go emotionally. They hold themselves back. This may be due to anxiety, fear, or shame in relation to sex or to intercourse itself. Some wives are afraid of being hurt; others are afraid of pregnancy. As excitement builds up, anxiety takes over and prevents complete release. All of the guilt and fear that have been built up over the years blocks response. Such negative feelings may slowly subside as time goes on, so the wife becomes less inhibited.

Inability to have an orgasm during coitus may also be due to distrust, anger, or resentment toward one's husband. Some wives feel too dependent, too open to being hurt or rejected. Dr. Arnold Lazarus writes:

> Some women equate the orgasmic experience with a frightening loss of control, or a type of surrender which produces unwanted vulnerability. To stop, just short of orgasm, keeps them "in the driver's seat." In one of my patients, this problem was based upon deep-seated resentment toward her husband to whom she did not wish to give the satisfaction "of knowing that he could give me pleasure." (Lazarus, 1975, p. 96)

A wife needs to be able to trust her husband completely, to be secure in his love and acceptance. If she is not, she holds back. Others wives have been hurt deeply, can't forget, so hold back in retaliation or as punishment.

Other wives are just the opposite. They want so much to please their husband that their thoughts are centered on their partner rather then on their own feelings and responses. Therapists call this *spectatoring:* being an observer rather than a participant. Of course, consideration for one's husband is helpful to a point, but quite detrimental to orgasm if overdone. One wife may worry that she's making her husband work too hard, so she urges him to come to a climax before she's satisfied. Another feels very self-conscious about being stimulated by her husband; she doesn't feel comfortable, because she is receiving and not giving. Another worries about what her husband will think of her if she really lets herself go: she's wondering whether or not he will lose respect, get mad, or reject her. Some wives feel very vulnerable, and quite helpless and dependent. They are afraid of losing their husband or of being abandoned. These fears interfere with their own responses. They don't dare let themselves go. In this situation, one of the goals of therapy would be to confront the wife with her own fears, to try to help her develop a new independence by going back to school or getting a job. The more secure she feels, the less sexually submissive she feels she has to be, and the more courage she feels in expecting her husband to try to satisfy her too. As one woman said: "He has his orgasm and pleasure, why shouldn't he expect to do the same for me?" What is suggested here is that the wife has to be able to feel enough self-confidence and security within herself to make justifiable demands upon her husband. She has a right to expect that he will try to satisfy her too.

TREATMENT

Diagnosis. The first task in treating the wife who has never experienced an orgasm (primary orgasmic dysfunction) is to find out whether she is suffering from orgastic inhibition, or whether she has never experienced an orgasm because she has not received sufficient and/or proper stimulation. If the latter is the cause, she and her husband can be instructed in pleasuring, sensate-focus techniques (see Chapter 5), masturbation, and coital positions, so that she can become sufficiently aroused to reach a climax. If orgasm incapacity has existed for some time, the couple may still exhibit considerable anxiety, guilt, disappointment, or intense anger that orgasm has not been forthcoming. Counseling is also needed to help the couple deal with these feelings.

Orgastic Inhibition. If it is found that the wife remains inorgastic even though stimulation through masturbation, love play, and coitus have been sufficient, it is evident that the problem is orgastic inhibition. The cause may be physical: she is taking drugs that sedate sexual response; an illness is blocking nerve transmission; she has a deficiency of androgens. As with other problems discussed in this book, all possible physical and medical factors should be checked out to discover if these are causing the problem. (See Chapter 3.) If they are not, the orgastic inhibition is psychological. The wife has learned to hold back, to control her sexual response, often unconsciously because of fear, guilt, conflict, hostility, or other negative feelings. These negative feelings may have arisen in the past in her associations with parents, siblings, or friends. They may have arisen in her present marriage out of uncertainty about the relationship, out of fear of losing her independence, out of hostility toward her mate. Whatever the cause, she is holding back, and nonorgasm is the result.

Achieving Orgasm. One important step is for the woman to achieve her first climax. Once she experiences this, part of her anxieties, disappointment, guilt, or anger will pass. Generally speaking, the first orgasm is usually achieved more easily through masturbation, particularly stimulation on and around the clitoral shaft. The husband may do this with her instruction, or she may do it herself while lying in his arms, or, if too embarrassed this way, by herself. If she cannot reach an orgasm manually, some therapists instruct her on the use of a vibrator.

Once orgasm is achieved through masturbation, the next step is to involve the husband in the masturbatory process, either manually, orally, or by using the vibrator, while guided by his wife's hand. The final step is achieving orgasm during coitus. This is more easily assured if heightened arousal takes place prior to intromission and if the clitoral area is stimulated manually during intercourse. Proper use of positions is also important, especially use of the female superior position as already discussed.

If the primary problem is in the husband-wife relationship, so the wife is situationally nonorgasmic with her husband because of negative feelings toward him, marriage counseling may be needed to help them work out their relationship. If the wife has quite deep-seated fears and anxieties, originating deep in her past, and if these are not overcome by performing the sexual tasks already described in Chapter 5, more lengthy psychotherapy may be needed to identify the roots of the difficulty and to remove these inhibitions.

However, before additional psychotherapy is instituted, it is better to check out the more immediate causes already discussed and to try to eliminate them. The inital focus needs to be on improving lovemaking techniques, breaking down inhibitions, enhancing communication. Even very disturbed marriages sometimes get surprisingly better once the couple's sexual relationship becomes satisfying and enjoyable to them both. Nothing is more thrilling than for a wife to have her first orgasm. She is filled with love and ecstasy. And nothing pleases a husband more than to be able to share this experience with her. It's a worthy goal.

17

DYSPAREUNIA
(PAINFUL INTERCOURSE)
AND VAGINISMUS

DYSPAREUNIA

Dyspareuina is painful coitus. In this condition, penile entry into the vagina is painful, pevlic thrusts are painful. If orgasm occurs, it is painful. Intercourse becomes an ordeal rather than a pleasure.

The following example is quite typical.

> I had a baby six months ago. Since then my husband and I have not been able to have intercourse very often because it hurts too much around the opening. My opening feels very tight, so that I have to use a lubricating jelly. My husband says I feel tighter too. When I had my six-week checkup my doctor said I was all right. If I am, then why does it hurt so much?

The fact that this wife began to have painful intercourse after pregnancy and childbirth when she had no difficulty before strongly suggested a medical rather than a psychological cause. Subsequent medical examinations revealed that in repairing the incision *(episiotomy)*, the tissues of the vaginal outlet were tightened excessively. In this case, the vaginal outlet was dilated initially by the doctor, and the wife was able to resume normal sexual relations soon after.

Physical Causes. Dyspareunia often has physical origins. One of the most frequently encountered causes is *lack of vaginal lubrication.* If the wife does not become sufficiently aroused prior to intercourse, the vagina remains dry. Under these circumstances, entry and intercourse can be painful.

Ordinarily, the vagina becomes lubricated during the excitement phase of sexual response. If vaginal lubrication does not occur, it may be that the wife has not become aroused. Without lubrication, the woman is not ready either physically or psychologically for intercourse. This is one reason why sufficient foreplay is essential: it prepares the wife mentally and physically to receive the erect penis. The answer therefore should be simple: make certain that arousal takes place ahead of time.

Unfortunately, however, this does not always work. After menopause, many women are not physically able to lubricate properly. As the ovaries cease production of their hormones, the vagina becomes thin and inelastic, gradually returning to its prepubertal state. In this condition, known as *senile vaginitis,* the thin walls crack, become irritated, and bleed easily. Under such circumstances, intercourse may become quite painful, especially since the natural lubricating mechanism also ceases to function properly. However, replacement therapy will correct the condition; but many doctors hesitate to prescribe hormones, or prefer not to for medical reasons. Under such circumstances, KY jelly or vaginal creams containing female hormones may be prescribed. It is helpful also if the wife uses the female superior position, where she has more control over the insertion of the penis into the vagina.

Of course, the actual causes of lack of lubrication may sometimes be psychological rather than physical. If the wife has lost affection and respect for her husband, and can no longer identify with him in a warm, responsive way, her dry vagina is but a symptom of her emotional rejection of him. Or if she fears pregnancy, pain, sexual inadequacy, or discovery, her natural responses, including her lubricating mechanism, will be inhibited. Or if a particular sexual experience is dirty, disgusting, or shameful for her, these feelings may inhibit all lubrication. A wife with lesbian orientations may lubricate with a female partner, but not with her husband.

Thus, even though the cause of pain is lack of lubrication, the reason for the insufficiency of vaginal secretion is psychological.

There are numerous other physical causes of dyspareunia. One of these is *physical abrasion and irritation,* often from frequent and lengthy intercourse. The following example is taken from the author's book on marriage.

> I am a newlywed four months and I should be used to making love since we do it every day. We can make love once, with no trouble, but if we do it the second or third time, I feel like pins are sticking into me, and intercourse becomes painful to the point of tears. We enjoy sex, but this is becoming a problem. Also, I keep getting infection after infection.

Two problems are illustrated in the above example. This young bride was suffering from what is commonly referred to as *honeymoon cystitis.* Frequent intercourse had irritated the vaginal opening, the clitoris, perhaps the urethra. The urethra is particularly subject to mechanical irritation. Since it is just above the vaginal opening, it may be pressed against the pubic bone during intercourse, caught between the penis and the pubis. Furthermore, during frequent sexual activity, it is easy for bacteria to enter the short urethral tube and enter the bladder. This can cause a urinary tract infection. Thus, the dual condition—mechanical irritation of the urethral opening and infection—may cause burning and painful intercourse. Many young brides complain of "burnys," of throbbing, of the feeling that they need to urinate frequently. In such cases, medical assistance is needed. Changing the position of intercourse so there is little or no pressure on the urethra is also helpful. One problem with this change in position, however, is that the clitoris also may not be stimulated, making orgasm more difficult, but this may be accomplished through manual manipulation during intercourse, as suggested in the last chapter.

Painful irritation may also be found in the clitoris itself. This may be due to a collection of smegma around the glans and beneath the clitoral hood. In such cases, the prepuce should be pulled back, and the glans cleaned. This is ordinarily necessary as a regular part of feminine hygiene, and illustrates the importance of keeping the genitalia clean.

Use of some *douches,* and especially of *contraceptive foams, creams, and jellies,* may also be irritating, particularly if large amounts are used frequently. Some women are more sensitive to these acid chemicals and cannot use them. Other women react painfully to the *rubber* or *plastic* that condoms and diaphragms are made of, or to excessive douching. Frequent douching may cause some women to become sensitive to the products used in the douching solution. Also, frequent douching disrupts the productive acid environment of the vagina, so that the woman is more subject to infections. For this reason, most doctors feel that routine douching after intercourse is unnecessary.

Other physical causes of dyspareunia are various *vaginal infections and funguses.* Common sources of vaginal infections are bacteria from the rectum, hands, clothing, or foreign substances pushed into the vagina. Fecal matter contains harmful bacteria which if introduced into the vagina may cause infection. This is common if either the finger or the penis is introduced into the anus and then into the vagina. The possibility of such infection is one of the strong arguments against anal intercourse. (See Chapter 9.) Of course, not all bacterial infections come from anal intercourse. Unclean hands or clothing may be contributing factors, which is another reason that strict attention should be paid to personal hygiene and cleanliness.

Some types of vaginal infections are by funguses (called *monilial infections*). These can cause swelling, weeping, burning, and itching of the tissues, so that urination and intercourse are painful. Untreated diabetes may predispose a woman to fungus infections. Whatever the cause of the infection, the assistance of a competent physician should be sought.

Injuries from childbirth are another source of painful intercourse. In some cases, scar tissue remains around the vaginal opening. Sometimes during an episiotomy vaginal muscles are cut and not properly repaired. Or there may be internal lacerations, tears, or lesions in the vaginal walls which cause pain. Masters and Johnson tell of treating eleven patients who had lacerations in the ligaments that support the uterus. Five of these tears were caused during childbirth, three by criminal abortions, and three by gang rape. All of these women were in need of surgical repair. (Masters and Johnson, 1970)

Two other causes of pain deep in the pelvis are *endometriosis* and *infections in the cervix, uterus, and Fallopian tubes.* Endometriosis is a condition in which the tissue that lines the uterus grows in other places in the pelvis. Infections of the cervix, etc., may be due to venereal disease, especially gonorrhea, or to other organisms found on the skin or in the colon. *Ovarian cysts* may cause pain, as may *retroversion of the uterus,* which leads to a *dislocation of the ovary.* In this case, the ovary is bumped by the thrusting penis. Sometimes pain occurs as an aftermath of an operation: for *cervical cancer,* for example.

In diagnosing the causes of dyspareunia, the physician will want to know the origin of the pain, whether it is localized around the vaginal opening, within the vaginal walls, or with deep penetration. Is the pain periodic, or does it occur every time the wife has intercourse? Is it episodic—for example, at the time of ovulation? Does it occur when the wife is highly aroused or when she is only mildly excited? Does it occur when the penis is first inserted, or does the pain increase with some vigorous penile thrusting? What were the circumstances surrounding the onset of the problem? Did it occur following childbirth, an operation, or a traumatic event? These and other questions will help the physician to diagnose the difficulty.

Psychological Causes. The same upsetting events or feelings that cause other problems of sexual dysfunction may also cause dyspareunia. For example, painful intercourse may be initiated by specific *traumatic events,* such as a discovery of the husband's infidelity or an emotional reaction to abortion. Or it may result from *fear of pregnancy* or *fear of sexual inadequacy.* It is not unusual to find new brides who are *afraid of being hurt,* especially as they contemplate having to accommodate their husband's erect penis. Mace writes:

> We all have a natural protective response to anyone who sticks things in our bodies; and an erect penis is a large object to have pushed deep into your insides. A nervous, apprehensive bride can easily react rather violently to this, even if she knows intellectually that the same thing happens to other women, and that the man who does it has the best of intentions. So long as the sense of apprehension lurks at the back of her mind, she can very easily persuade herself that she is being physically hurt, especially if her husband's movements are vigorous. It is worthwhile to take time to give the wife plenty of understanding, reassurance, and support, until her fears vanish and she can welcome intercourse as a pleasant experience. (Mace, 1972, p. 41)

Treatment. Treatment will depend, of course, partially on whether the problem has a physical or a psychological origin. Since physical causes are so common, the assistance of a competent physician should be the first step. Rarely is surgery needed. Many times, medications are prescribed. Vaginal creams are often suggested to assure lubrication and minimize discomfort. In some cases of vaginal lesions or tears, Hartman and Fithian prescribe vaginal exercises that fill in the muscle so that intercourse is no longer painful. They also prescribe these exercises for those with loose vaginas or for those who are having difficulty in having orgasm during intercourse. Very briefly, the exercises consist of tightening and loosening the so-called *pubococcygeus muscle* 25 to 50 times a day. The woman can identify the muscle by sitting on the toilet, her legs as far apart as possible, and feeling the muscle work as she stops and starts the flow of urine. The pubococcygeus muscle is the only muscle that can stop the flow of urine in this position. (Hartman and Fithian, 1972, p. 88) Hartman and Fithian ask all the women they work with to learn to contract and to hold the muscle tight for 3 seconds at a time, and then to relax it, and to do this 25 to 50 times daily.

Sensate-focus treatment is also used for painful intercourse when the problems are psychogenic in origin. Similar procedures are followed as for other female sexual dysfunctions. (See Chapter 5.) Marriage counseling and psychotherapy may also be needed to deal with negative emotions and feelings.

VAGINISMUS

It has been said that the woman with dyspareunia really hurts, but the woman with vaginismus fears that she may be hurt. *Vaginismus is actually an involuntary spastic contraction of the muscles surrounding the vaginal entrance.* The contraction occurs whenever penile penetration is attempted and may be so severe that it is painful. Under such circumstances, intercourse is impossible. Masters and Johnson treated one patient who had not had intercourse for the first fourteen years of marriage because of this condition. (Belliveau and Richter, 1970, p. 184)

One sure way to be certain that vaginismus is present is through physical examination. Characteristically, the woman will attempt to slide up to the head of the examining table when approached by the doctor, even taking her feet out of the stirrups and keeping her legs together. Calm reassurance is needed before the doctor examines her. When the doctor attemps to insert one finger into the vagina, the muscles immediately close, preventing the finger from entering.

Many women who seek treatment for vaginismus are actually sexually responsive. They enjoy sexual contact and sexual play, and can have an orgasm with clitoral stimulation, as long as this does not lead to intercourse. But whenever any attempt at vaginal penetration is made, the efforts evoke intense fear, upset, and rage, with the feelings subsiding only when the "danger" of entry is removed. Usually, the wife is frightened, frustrated, and ashamed of her reactions, which are not under her voluntary control. As might be expected, she tries to avoid intercourse completely.

Husbands' reactions are important and varied. If the husband tries to enter her forcibly, the problem usually gets worse. The wife's pain increases, so the next time entry is more difficult than ever. Most husbands feel frustrated and rejected. Some are able to accept sex play and noncoital sex as substitutes, some are not. Some husbands eventually develop secondary impotence as a reaction to their wife's problem.

Causes. Vaginismus may develop only after a long toleration of painful intercourse. Such physical causes as the presence of scar tissue, lesions and tears in the vaginal walls or in the broad ligaments supporting the uterus, endometriosis, ovarian cysts, or postmenopausal vaginitis which make intercourse painful may be the prelude to vaginismus. The wife is not able to tolerate the pain of intercourse any longer, and begins to develop vaginismus. Even after the physical causes have been corrected, reconditioning may be needed to help her overcome her fear reactions of being hurt.

Some women have developed vaginismus after traumatic experiences, particularly after sexual molestation, assault, or gang rape. In other cases, it develops out of a family background in which sex is considered sinful, dirty, and incompatible with religious beliefs. Twelve of the 29 women with vaginismus who were reported in Masters and Johnson's book came from this kind of family. (Masters and Johnson, 1970) The woman whose marriage had not been consummated for fourteen years came from a family whose attitudes about sex were completely negative. The father and the mother both were very strict disciplinarians. Anything having to do with sex was taboo. The girl was not allowed to look at her breasts while bathing. Discussion of menstruation, intercourse, having babies, or contraception was not allowed. Before marriage, her physical contact with her fiancé had consisted of a few kisses, with someone else present. She was married without any counseling about sexual matters except that her priest told her that intercourse could be tolerated for procreation only.

The husband was brought up with a similar background. The honeymoon was traumatic, with the marriage never consummated. The only sexual contact at all was when the wife masturbated her husband, which was once or twice a week. (Belliveau and Richter, 1970, p. 187)

Quite commonly, also, wives with vaginismus are married to impotent men. Whether the vaginismus causes the impotency, or vice versa, may not always be known, but if the husband attempts intercourse over a period of time and his wife screams or cries when penetration is attempted, the husband may lose his erection. If this happens frequently, the impotency may be well established. Of course one could say also that if the wife reacts negatively, defensively to her husband's impotence, it is possible that vaginismus could develop as her defensive reaction to his problem. Of course, her negative reaction may be her way of rejecting him. Mace has suggested that the woman who unconsciously closes her vagina to her husband is saying in effect: "I am afraid to let you come fully into my life by opening myself freely and trustfully to you." (Mace, 1971) If the marital relationship has become very disturbed, or if the husband has been inconsiderate or even brutal in his sexual approaches to his wife, she may very well develop vaginismus as a result.

Treatment. Assuming that all physical causes have been corrected first, the treatment approach to vaginismus is incredibly simple: it is to eliminate gradually the woman's fear reaction to the insertion of the penis into her vagina by the introduction, under relaxed conditions, of objects of gradually increasing size into her vagina. (Kaplan, 1975, p. 99) When the woman can tolerate an object the size of a penis, she is cured.

Various therapists use different objects. Some recommend graduated glass catheters; others use rubber; and still others use a tampon. Dr. Helen Kaplan uses the patient's and the husband's finger only, because she has found these to be more emotionally acceptable to patients who tend to resist artificial objects. (Kaplan, 1975, p. 100) Kaplan instructs the woman to observe her vaginal entrance in a mirror when she is by herself. She is asked to place her index finger at the vaginal outlet and to see the reactions of the muscles. Gradually, she is able to insert her fingertip, then the whole finger, then two fingers. Sometimes she is asked to use a tampon and to leave it there for several hours until it feels comfortable. (Kaplan, 1975, p. 109)

After the woman feels comfortable inserting her fingers, the husband is then asked to repeat the procedure she has previously carried out: fingertip, whole finger, two fingers, then moving the finger, then two fingers, gently in and out. After the wife can accept this, the penis is well lubricated and penetration takes place while she guides him. The husband leaves his penis in quietly, without thrusting, then withdraws. The final steps are gentle thrusting, then finally thrusting to orgasm.

Counseling and psychotherapy are an important part of the whole process: to discover the reasons for the onset of vaginismus, particularly the influence of traumatic events. It is not difficult for the wife to understand how trauma or pain may have initiated the problem. Negative childhood conditioning may take fairly lengthy psychotherapy to change basic attitudes and feelings. If disturbed marital relationships are making the wife react to her husband, then marital counseling may be needed. If the husband has developed impotency, then his problem has to be treated also. (See Chapter 12.)

Belliveau and Richter write:

> While it is relatively easy to deal with the physical aspect of vaginismus, the emotional aspect must be treated also. There is no question that relief of the physical distress leaves the emotional problems more amenable to treatment. The therapists take the opportunity above all to inform these women of what they can legitimately expect from their sexual lives. Women who have been inhibited by religious sanctions, who are married to impotent men, who have been traumatized by rape or by severely painful intercourse or are otherwise emotionally damaged from whatever cause must be helped to allow themselves a sexual existence. (Belliveau and Richter, 1970, p. 193)

Masters and Johnson have been outstandingly successful in treating vaginismus. All of the women originally treated by them, and reported in their book, were able to overcome the problem. Twenty-two had orgasm for the first time in their lives. Six who were secondarily nonorgasmic were able again to reach a climax. Only three were not able to have an orgasm even though the vaginismus was gone. (Belliveau and Richter, 1970, p. 194) Kaplan also reports virtually 100 percent success in treatment. (Kaplan, 1975)

PART V

SEX
THERAPY

18

GETTING HELP

MEDICAL HELP

Probably the best place to begin is with one's own physician. It's usually not possible for the lay person to determine whether the cause of a sexual difficulty has a physical origin or an emotional or psychological basis, so there is wisdom in selecting a medical doctor first. However, some physicians are well qualified to diagnose the causes of sexual difficulties and some are not. I always admire the man who will admit straight out if he doesn't feel qualified and will recommend a specialist. Unfortunately, there are some physicians who will attempt to deal with sexual difficulties when, in fact, they are not knowledgeable. In the past, there was little or nothing in the medical school curriculum about treating sexual inadequacy, so that the average senior physician today has neither the training nor the time to get involved in dealing with sexual problems. However, the picture is slowly changing, so that tomorrow's doctor will be better trained. As of now, however, many physicians are wise if they refer their patients.

Referrals are made to different kinds of specialists. Most often, women are referred to a *gynecologist,* men are referred to a *urologist.* If general diagnosis is required, the first referral may be to an *internist,* who specializes in internal medicine and diagnosis. If hormonal difficulties are suspected, the physician may recommend an *endocrinologist.*

Nervous disorders are treated by a *neurologist.* If deep-seated emotional problems are suspected, the referral may be to a *psychiatrist.*

However, within these various specialties, there are physicians who are quite knowledgeable about sexual dysfunction and those who are not. One would think that since so many women take their sexual problems to a gynecologist, for example, all gynecologists would be experts at treating this type of disorder. However, since this is not the case, many of these specialists themselves refer women to other physicians who are experts in this field. It is difficult to tell by the specialty whether an individual will be most helpful or not. Some urologists become experts at dealing with problems of impotency or ejaculatory incompetence in men, others not. Some psychiatrists become experts in the type of sex therapy discussed in this book; others use very traditional psychoanalysis which may or may not be needed. A call to the local or state medical association may provide some clues as to where to go if the help or suggestions of the family physician do not suffice.

SEX THERAPISTS

In the past, it was the usual practice for the physician to recommend that patients go to a psychiatrist if emotional problems were suspected. Of course, this procedure is still followed by many and is needed in some cases. But it has been found that symptom-focused sex therapy does more good in a much shorter period of time than psychiatric treatment, unless deep psychological problems are at the root of the problem which prevents sex therapy from working. What is needed is the help of an expert in this type of sex therapy. Sex therapists may be psychiatrists, but just as often they are marriage or sex counselors, often with a background in psychology or in marriage and family relationships, but with specialized training in sex therapy in addition. The American Association of Sex Educators, Counselors, and

Therapists maintains an active list of certified sex therapists. This organization should be consulted for recommendations within one's own area. Write: American Association of Sex Educators, Counselors, and Therapists, 5010 Wisconsin Avenue N.W., Suite 304, Washington, D.C. 20016.

Unfortunately, many untrained, unqualified persons have set themselves up as "sex counselors." One hears stories of counselors who become sexually involved with their patients, who demonstrate lovemaking techniques by showing clients in person how to make love. Others insist that couples disrobe and practice in front of them. This is not necessary. Masters and Johnson, Kaplan, and other qualified therapists instruct couples in pleasuring and sensate-focus techniques, but ask couples to perform these sexual tasks in the privacy of their own bedroom, or in a motel room if the couple are away from home. For the counselor to become physically or emotionally involved with clients in any way will only add to the confusion, anxiety, and turmoil of the client. It is significant that many therapists will work only as a co-therapy team, with a man and a woman together. There are some highly competent therapists who work alone, but all therapists use conjoint therapy—they insist on seeing the husband and the wife together, since the goal is to instruct them both on how to find sexual fulfillment, how to improve their sexual response and communication and their total relationship. Couples are given "assignments," which are completed privately, not in front of the therapists.

Of course, many times physical examinations are required, but these should be done by professionally qualified physicians. Sometimes, a physician will ask the husband or the wife to be a part of the examination. For example, one way to help the husband understand his wife's problem of vaginismus is to observe a gynecological examination. But this is handled in a professional way, like any other medical examination. Couples have to be aware that there are highly qualified therapists and there are some quacks. So before deciding, the couple must talk to that person or persons to find out more about the therapists' background and training, general philosophy, approach, and procedures. Not all therapists operate exactly according to some of the descriptions in this book. New techniques are being developed all the time which are improvements over old ones. Also, each therapist has his or her own way of proceeding, but clients have the right ahead of time to know what to expect. If in doubt, they can check with local better business bureaus, medical associations, family planning agencies, mental health clinics, family service organizations, clergymen or church organizations, social service organizations, or the psychology department of a local university to find out as much about individual counselors as possible.

MARRIAGE COUNSELORS

Some marriage counselors are also sex therapists; others refer clients with problems of sexual dysfunction, especially if these problems do not seem to be marriage-oriented. The American Association of Marriage and Family Counselors keeps an up-to-date list of certified members. Write to the national headquarters: American Association of Marriage and Family Counselors, 6211 W. Northwest Highway, Dallas, Tex. 75225, and enclose a stamped, self-addressed return envelope and they will give you the names of members in your locality. The certification requirements are stringent, so most members should be quite competent.

Of course, there are many fine marriage counselors who are not members. These include some clergy, social workers, psychologists, and others. The two community agencies that are likely to provide professional marriage counseling services are the Family Service Agency and the Community Counseling Center. In addition, the Yellow Pages provide a list under the heading "Marriage and Family Counselors." However, in most states, any person can claim to be a marriage counselor, get a business phone and a listing in the Yellow Pages and be in business. No license or certification or even a college degree is needed to start private practice in most states. For this reason, couples ought to check out the education and credentials of any counselor they are thinking of going to before they make a decision.

Many individual professionals do an excellent job of marriage counseling. Clergymen who have specialized training, and especially if they are clinical members of the American Association of Pastoral Counselors, are very good, but it is hard to know about individuals. Clergymen in every community need to search for the best people to whom to refer parishioners. Since most fair-sized cities have one or more pastors who are also expert marriage counselors, it is helpful if other clergy become acquainted with them and try to make arrangements for referral of their parishioners. By combining resources, people can be better served.

In a college community, professors of marriage and family life education, human sexuality, counseling, or psychology sometimes do private counseling on the side or can refer people to competent professionals, so their advice might be sought.

There is no particular profession that has all of the qualified sex therapists or marriage counselors. Many different professions produce a few really outstanding counselors. All that any couple can do is seek out the very best. If a particular counselor is not helping after a considerable period of time, it's better to switch than to remain troubled and disappointed.

BIBLIOGRAPHY

Ard, Ben N., Jr. *Treating Psychosexual Dysfunction.* Jason Aronson, Inc., 1974.

Bell, Robert R. "Some Emerging Sexual Expectations Among Women." In *The Social Dimension of Human Sexuality,* edited by Robert R. Bell and Michael Gordon. Little, Brown & Company, 1972.

Bell, Robert R., and Bell, P. L. "Sexual Satisfaction Among Married Women." *Medical Aspects of Human Sexuality,* December 1972, pp. 136–144.

Bell, Robert R., and Connolly, J. "Non-Coital Sex in Marriage." Toronto: National Council on Family Relations, October 1973.

Belliveau, Fred, and Richter, Lin. *Understanding Human Sexual Inadequacy.* Bantam Books, Inc., 1970.

"Birth Control Deaths." *Newsweek,* March 1, 1976, p. 60.

Bullock, R. C., *et al.* "The Weeping Wife: Marital Relations of Depressed Women." *Journal of Marriage and the Family,* 34 (August 1972): 488–495.

Catholic Theological Society of America, Committee on the Study of Human Sexuality. *Human Sexuality, New Directions in American Catholic Thought.* Paulist Press, 1977.

Clayton, George. "The Contemporary Experience of Adultery: Bob and Carol and Updike and Rimmer." In *Renovating Marriage,* edited by Roger W. Libby and Robert N. Whitehurst. Consensus Publishers, Inc., 1973.

Constantine, Larry L., and Constantine, Joan M. *Group Marriage.* Collier Books, 1974.

Cuber, John, and Harroff, Peggy B. *The Significant Ameri-*

cans: A Study of Sexual Behavior Among the Affluent.
Appleton-Century-Crofts, 1965.

DeBurger, James E. "Marital Problems, Help-Seeking and Emotional Orientation as Revealed in Help-Request Letters." *Journal of Marriage and the Family,* 29 (November 1967):712–721.

Denfeld, Duane. "Dropouts from Swinging: The Marriage Counselor as Informant." In *Beyond Monogamy,* edited by James R. Smith and Lynn G. Smith. The Johns Hopkins University Press, 1974.

Ehrlich, Richard M. "Impotence Associated with Prostatitis." In *Medical Aspects of Human Sexuality,* edited by Harold I. Lief. The Williams & Wilkins Co., 1975.

Fisher, Seymour. *The Female Orgasm: Psychology, Physiology, Fantasy.* Basic Books, Inc., 1973.

Flowers, Charles E. "Sex Relations After Hysterectomy." In *Medical Aspects of Human Sexuality,* edited by Harold I. Lief. The Williams & Wilkins Co., 1975.

Freud, Sigmund. "Three Essays on the Theory of Sexuality." In *Standard Edition,* Vol. III. London: Hogarth Press, Ltd., 1953.

Gebhard, P. S. "Factors in Marital Orgasm." *The Journal of Social Issues,* 22 (1966):88–95.

Gilmartin, B. G., and Kusisto, D. V. "Some Personal and Social Characteristics of Mate-Sharing Swingers." In *Renovating Marriage,* edited by Roger W. Libby and Robert N. Whitehurst. Consensus Publishers, Inc., 1973.

Greenblatt, Robert B. "Steroid Replacement and Libido." In *Medical Aspects of Human Sexuality,* edited by Harold I. Lief. The Williams & Wilkins Co., 1975.

Greiff, B. "Occupational Setback and Impotence." In *Medical Aspects of Human Sexuality,* edited by Harold I. Lief. The Williams & Wilkins Co., 1975.

Hartman, William E., and Fithian, Marilyn A. *Treatment of Sexual Dysfunction: A Bio-Psycho/Social Approach.* Long Beach, Calif.: Center for Marital and Sexual Studies, 1972.

Hite, Shere. *The Hite Report: A Nationwide Study on Female Sexuality.* Dell Publishing Co., Inc., 1977.

Humphrey, F. G. "Study Says Adultery Is Serious Problem." *Portland Press Herald,* April 11, 1977.

Kanter, Rosabeth M. *Commitment and Community: Communes and Utopias in Sociological Perspective.* Harvard University Press, 1972.

Kaplan, Helen S. *The Illustrated Manual of Sex Therapy.* Quadrangle/The New York Times Book Co., 1975.

Kaplan, Helen S. *The New Sex Therapy.* London: Baillière, Tindall, 1974.

Kinsey, Alfred C., *et al. Sexual Behavior in the Human Female.* W. B. Saunders Company, 1953.

Kinsey, Alfred C., *et al. Sexual Behavior in the Human Male.* W. B. Saunders Company, 1948.

Kolodny, Robert C. "Androgens to Increase Female Libido." In *Medical Aspects of Human Sexuality,* edited by Harold I. Lief. The Williams & Wilkins Co., 1975.

Landis, Judson T., and Landis, Mary G. *Building a Successful Marriage.* 6th ed. Prentice-Hall, Inc., 1973.

Lazarus, Arnold A. "Female Fear of Orgasm." In *Medical Aspects of Human Sexuality,* edited by Harold I. Lief. The Williams & Wilkins Co., 1975.

Levin, Robert J., and Levin, A. "Sexual Pleasure: The Surprising Preferences of 100,000 Women." *Redbook,* September 1975, pp. 51–58.

Mace, David. *Sexual Difficulties in Marriage.* Fortress Press, 1972.

Mace, David. "Sexual Marital Enrichment." In *The New Sexuality,* edited by Herbert A. Otto. Science and Behavior Books, Inc., 1971.

Masters, William H., and Johnson, Virginia E. *Human Sexual Inadequacy.* Little, Brown & Company, 1970.

Masters, William H., and Johnson, Virginia E. *Human Sexual Response.* Little, Brown & Company, 1966.

Masters, William H., and Johnson, Virginia E. *The Pleasure Bond: A New Look at Sexuality and Commitment.* Bantam Books, Inc., 1976.

Mathews, V. D., and Mihanovich, Clement S. "New Orientations on Marital Adjustment." *Marriage and Family Living,* 25 (August 1963):300–304.

McCary, James Leslie. *Human Sexuality.* 2d ed. Van Nostrand-Reinhold Company, 1973.

Morrison, Eleanor S., and Borosage, Vera (eds.). *Human Sex-*

uality: Contemporary Perspectives. National Press Books,
1973.

"Notable Success Reported with Sex Drugs." *Portland Press
Herald,* July 30, 1977.

O'Connor, J. F., and Stern, L. O. "Results of Treatment in
Functional Sexual Disorders." *New York State Journal of
Medicine,* 72 (1972):1927–1934.

O'Neill, Nena, and O'Neill, George. *Open Marriage.* Avon
Books, 1973.

Pearlman, C. K. "Frequency of Intercourse in Males at Different Ages." *Medical Aspects of Human Sexuality,* November 1972, pp. 92–113.

Peters, J. J. "Emotional Recovery from Rape." In *Medical
Aspects of Human Sexuality,* edited by Harold I. Lief. The
Williams & Wilkins Co., 1975.

Reik, Theodor. *Psychology of Sex Relations.* Rinehart &
Company, Inc., 1945.

Reuben, David R. *Everything You Always Wanted to Know
About Sex.* Bantam Books, Inc., 1971.

Rice, F. Philip. *Marriage and Parenthood.* Allyn & Bacon,
Inc. Forthcoming.

Sherfey, Mary Jane. *The Nature and Evolution of Female
Sexuality.* Vintage Books, Inc., 1973.

Sigusch, V., *et al.* "Psychosexual Stimulation: Sex Differences." *Journal of Sex Research,* 6 (February 1970):10–24.

Varni, C. "Contents of Conversion: The Case of Swinging."
In *Renovating Marriage,* edited by Roger W. Libby and
Robert N. Whitehurst. Consensus Publishers, Inc., 1973.